the common sense of

TOM PAINE

*Some other biographies by Richard O'Connor
for young people*

JOHN LLOYD STEPHENS
Explorer of Lost Civilizations

SITTING BULL
War Chief of the Sioux

YOUNG BAT MASTERSON

the common sense of

TOM PAINE

by Richard O'Connor

Illustrated by Richard Cuffari

McGRAW-HILL BOOK COMPANY

New York • Toronto • San Francisco

Contents

cop. 2

the common sense of
TOM PAINE

The Boy Who Asked Questions

I

THE Reverend William Knowles was a stern-looking young man with a sense of duty toward the boys he taught in his spare time at the grammar school in the village of Thetford. He was tall and straight-backed. He had served in the Royal Navy and believed in the value of discipline, but he was also quick to single out and prize the unusual boy, the one who did not conform. Most of his pupils, in the fall of 1745, were destined for hard-working lives as farmers and workmen, but there was one who showed promise of being different.

That one had written a scrawl over which the Reverend Knowles was frowning. It was signed "Thomas Paine." Young Master Paine was a rare boy who asked questions and was not always satisfied with the answers.

Tom was the son of a corset-maker, and the Reverend

Knowles knew that he would not be content to follow his father into that trade.   There was a danger that the boy would become known as a troublemaker.   And that, as everyone knew, was the first step on the road to the gallows.

There was a knock on the door, not a timid one.

"Enter," said the teacher, clearing his throat.

A small boy marched into the room.   He had dark unruly hair, dark brown eyes quizzical and defiant in turn, and a long nose that looked as though it belonged on someone older.

"You sent for me, sir?" the boy asked.   "I'm Tom Paine."

His voice did not quiver with fear as most boys' did when they were summoned to the teacher's study.

"I know you well, Master Paine," the Reverend Knowles replied.   "Yes, I did send for you."   He tapped the paper in front of him.   "This . . . this bit of doggerel is yours?"

It was evidently a new word to him, and the boy's eyes were suddenly alive with curiosity.   "What's *doggerel,* sir?" he asked.

"Bad poetry, my lad.   Yesterday," the Reverend Knowles recalled, "I asked you to submit a paper expressing the beauties of the English countryside, this Norfolk, your native heath."

"Yes, sir," Tom Paine agreed.

"And this is what you handed in."   The teacher shoved the paper across the desk.   "Read it aloud . . . if you can bear to."

Tom picked up the paper, then slowly read:

[*10*]

Here lies the body of John Crow,
Who once was high, but now is low;
Ye brother crows, take warning all,
For as ye rise, so must ye fall.

There was silence in the room when Tom finished. The Reverend Knowles turned slightly in his chair to stare out the window. Tom was trying to decide what to do with the paper in his hands.

Outside the windows an autumn rain was steadily falling on the brown fields. A flight of rooks arrowed across the gray leaden skies. It had been drizzling for days and looked as though it would continue until the first snow.

The teacher asked, "How old are you, Master Paine?"

"Eight, sir."

"Old enough to be going to work soon. Time to be thinking about what you're going to make of your life. Why did you write that poem about the crow?"

"It just came to me, sir."

"Inspiration?" the Reverend Knowles asked, trying not to smile.

"It was raining out, like today," Tom explained. "There was nothing beautiful to describe. Then my pet crow died and I wrote that as his epitaph."

"I see," the Reverend Knowles said, nodding. "It does point a moral, after all. I suppose it's not too bad for a boy who will spend his life making corsets for the ladies of the town."

"Oh, I won't be doing that, sir," Tom confidently replied.

"No? Perhaps you'll be managing the estates of the Duke of Grafton?"

The boy shook his head. "I am going to be a writer."

"A writer! Already you've promoted yourself into the gentry!" The teacher suddenly recalled his own boyish hopes of becoming First Sea Lord of the Royal Navy, and his tone was gentler. "Don't aim too high. Thwarted hopes have a way of making men rebels. Now go home and write me an essay on the Norfolk countryside, and leave out the dead crows!"

The boy slipped out of the room. Nothing the Rev. Mr. Knowles had said changed his mind. Nothing anybody could say would ever turn Tom Paine from a path he intended to take.

There were few in Thetford who would have disagreed with the Reverend Knowles's forebodings about Tom Paine. In the England of the eighteenth century, you followed your father's footsteps and hoped for nothing better. Yet in that English market town there now stands a bronze plaque donated by members of the United States Air Force who were stationed at a nearby base during World War II. It pays tribute, as the plaque reads, to Tom Paine, "this simple son of England who lives on through the ideals and principles of this democratic world for which we fight today" and to "the everlasting love of freedom embodied in his works."

Paine rebelled against the political and social systems of his time exactly because they presumed to cut the pattern for a man's life according to the circumstances of his birth rather than the talents he might develop. He wanted men to be free to determine their own course. Without that rebellion, as the second American President John Adams said, there would have been no American Revolution.

His life began on January 29, 1737. In a small stone house on White Hart Street, in the town of Thetford, Tom Paine was born to Joseph and Frances Paine.

Very early the boy was aware of differences and disagreements in the small whitewashed house where he was raised and where his father made corsets for the ladies of the town.

The main differences were between his father and mother and between Tom and his parents. His father was a Quaker and worked with his hands. He was eleven years younger than Tom's mother. Mrs. Paine was the daughter of a lawyer and therefore higher on the social scale, a member of the Church of England, and bitter with her own disappointments. Rather than not getting married at all, it was said, she had married beneath her.

Because of those differences, it was not a happy home. Being raised as a Quaker, like his father, set Tom apart from other boys. Quakers refused to serve in the army and were looked down upon by everyone else. Until recently, in fact, they had been persecuted for their religion both in England and Germany, and many were forced to migrate to America.

His early life might have been happier if he had had brothers and sisters. A year after Tom's arrival, his mother gave birth to a baby girl. But Tom's sister died a few months later, and there were no other children.

He was often lonely, without playmates. The other boys would chase him away when he tried to join in their games, throwing sticks and stones at him and shouting, "Quack, quack, Quaker! Quack, quack, Quaker!" At school he was also set apart because he could not study Latin as the other boys did. Learning Latin was forbidden to Quaker boys.

Very soon he grew to hate the town where he was born. Its streets were rivers of mud when it rained. The houses were all stone boxes built right up to the street. It was a town of 2,000 when he was a boy, but after dark it was gloomy as a prison, with only an occasional window mellow with candlelight.

His silent, inward-looking father loved him, as Tom would learn when he was older, but had little time or energy for anything but corset-making. Work and sleep, that was Joseph Paine's daily routine. Was that all Tom himself could hope for when he grew up—to be an extra pair of hands snipping out bits and pieces of material for corset-making?

"What if I don't *want* to make corsets?" Tom asked his mother one day shortly after the Rev. Mr. Knowles had tried to dampen his ambition to be a writer. "What if I want to be a poet?"

His mother's sharp gray eyes studied him briefly.

"You'll have no choice," she said. "Your path is marked for you just as the Duke of Grafton's is for him. The only other path leads to prison or the gallows."

"I want to find my own path," the boy said stubbornly. "Suppose I wanted to be a lawyer like Grandfather?"

More gently, she replied, "My father's father was also a lawyer. It was easy enough for him. But *your* father is a corset-maker, and you will make corsets. That's the way life is, Thomas. We have no choice. Now, stop asking questions and draw me a bucket of water before it gets dark." Though Mrs. Paine's father had not disowned her for marrying Joseph Paine, he would not lift a finger to help his grandson.

On his way to the well, Tom passed through the front room, which served as his father's shop.

In the fading light his father was sewing fancy stitches into a corset attached to an iron-ribbed frame built to resemble a woman's torso. Around him on the floor were scraps of the linen, calico, silk, and linsey-woolsey used in making corsets. Joseph Paine spent all his days straining his eyes and working his fingers to the bone over sewing bits of fabric together. Was that any better than prison, the gallows, or the workhouse?

Tom refused to believe it. From the books he studied in school and those he could borrow from the Reverend Knowles, he was learning of a wider, more exciting and adventurous world than that of Thetford, where people were content with their daily bread and beer. An outside world where a man could better himself if he had the courage to try. . . .

When he reached the age of thirteen, the local grammar school had taught him all he was supposed to know— enough to make a living as his father's apprentice.

As a citizen of Thetford, all other thinking would be done for him by the Duke of Grafton. The town was part of a borough politically dominated by the Duke. There were only thirty-two men among all of Thetford's 2,000 who had the right to vote in an election and they voted the way the Duke of Grafton told them to vote. The Duke was a member of the Whig party and the Whigs ran the government and treated the national treasury as though it were their own property.

Even in his early teens Tom Paine objected to the system. He would be required to pay taxes but he would have no say in how they were used. He had to obey the laws which the Duke and his friends passed, but he had no part in framing them. Was he any better than a slave?

It did not seem so to Tom when he left school at thirteen. He could still dream of the outside world and its opportunities, but his help was required in his father's shop. Instead of studying, he now spent his days learning how to make corsets. His father's customers would come to be fitted, and Tom would take their measurements with a tape. Then he and his father would work away at cloth and whalebone. It was tiresome work and Tom hated it, especially when he had to be polite to ladies who looked down their noses at him.

Occasionally, as a relief from the boredom of his days and the gloom of his home, his father's constant talk of religion and his mother's sharp tongue, he would escape to the fields and moors outside Thetford. Or he would walk through the unlighted streets at night for a visit to the vicarage. The Rev. Mr. Knowles had quit schoolteaching and was now the vicar of the church his mother attended.

Tom Paine and the minister had become good friends. They could talk about books and the outside world, in which most of their fellow citizens had little interest. Recalling his days in the Royal Navy, the Reverend often told Tom, "It's a great life for a young man. You taste real freedom at sea, within the limits of naval discipline.

Aboard a fighting ship you get a lifetime of adventure in a few years. You see distant lands, far-off ports and strange peoples.

"I can always remember the dawns on a southern sea, the nights when the only sound came from the wind filling the sails—days when we hove to with other ships of the line and faced the enemy with thundering broadsides—nights when we celebrated a victory and thanked God we were alive after the perils of battle . . . and when I remember this, the day is not dull."

No doubt the Reverend Knowles's tales of naval adventure had mellowed with the passing years. Tom had too quick a mind to swallow them whole. But it still seemed to the boy that the sea offered him a possible means of escape from unending years of cutting bits of cloth and fitting them to stubborn lengths of whalebone.

The hopelessness and petty cruelty of life in a dull country town were brought home to him one Sunday on his way to church. A young girl had been put in the stocks, trussed up on a wooden frame until she fainted from the pain.

When he returned home, he asked his father, "How can we let such things happen and call ourselves Christians, even Quakers?"

Joseph Paine always spoke in the Biblical thee-and-thou of his faith. " 'Tis God's will," he told his seventeen-year-old son. "The girl spoke saucily to her father, and her father asked the authorities that she be punished."

"Then it wasn't God's will, but her father's," Tom angrily replied.

"Thou must not be disrespectful," his father said.

[*17*]

"The girl might die! Is that a fit punishment for speaking 'saucily'?"

"Go to thy room," the elder Paine said harshly. "And thou shalt stay there until thou hast prayed for forgiveness and known a change of heart."

Tom went up to his room under the eaves and stayed there all day. He did not go downstairs to supper. A little later he heard his parents retiring for the night. All that time Tom was thinking, not about his sin in defying his father, but about Thetford, the girl in the stocks, the people (including himself) who walked past her unconscious form with only a side glance.

Late that night he climbed out the narrow window to the slate roof, then dropped nimbly to the ground. With him he carried only one of his few possessions, a book titled *A Natural History of Virginia,* which was a gift from the Reverend Knowles.

Away to Sea

2

IT WAS thirty miles from Thetford to the port of Harwich.
Tom, carrying his book about the New World, walked most
of the night and the next day in order to reach the water-
front.

Late in the afternoon he limped along the wharves of
Harwich. He asked about the ships in port. A bearded
sailor wearing one gold earring and carrying a parrot on his
shoulder told Tom that the privateer *Terrible* was signing
on a new crew and preparing to sail on another foray.

In that year of 1754 France and England were fighting
an undeclared war, mostly on the high seas. For decades
the French and English had been warring, off and on, over
the attempt of the English to extend their influence over
parts of western Europe. In the present conflict, each nation concentrated on seizing the other's merchant ships at

sea.   The *Terrible* was one of the English ships engaged in raiding the French shipping lanes.

It was a grim and merciless and silent war about which Tom knew little, except that it offered adventure.

With eager anticipation he walked up the gangway of the *Terrible* and asked a boatswain leaning against the rail who the captain was.   The sailor grinned and replied: "Our captain is Death.   Captain Death, my lad.   And I can tell you he lives up to his name where the Frenchies are concerned.   Looking for excitement, boy?   Well, then, follow me!"

Only a few minutes after being shown into Captain Death's cabin, Tom signed on as a member of the *Terrible's* crew.   Next he went below and ate his first square meal in two days. As he was finishing, he was summoned back to the captain's cabin.

Awaiting his arrival with the captain was his father. Joseph Paine had set out in pursuit of his son as soon as he realized that Tom had run away.   His face was sad.

"Why did thee run away, Tom?"

"You must know, Father, that I won't be content with making corsets the rest of my life."

"But thou art the son of a Quaker," the elder Paine pointed out.   "What dost thou know of the horrors of war?   What dost thou know of the hardships endured by men at sea?"

"I am a man," Tom replied in a subdued voice.   "I expect to go through my share of danger."

"God will allot thy share."   Joseph Paine turned to the captain.   "Thou art a good man, despite thy calling. Tell my son—"

[22]

"I ran away to sea myself, lad," Captain Death said. "Your father's right. The sea is for those who have no other place to go. Anyway," he added gruffly, "you're too young for my crew."

"Come home with me, Tom," his father urged.

Tom said nothing. His father's face was haggard. Against his yearnings for the excitement of the world outside Thetford he had to balance his father's sorrow. He wondered if life would always offer a succession of such hard choices.

"Thou art my only son," the elder Paine said quietly. "I love thee more than I may sometimes show. Will thou come home with me?"

Finally Tom nodded. He cared about his father more than he could show.

The captain agreed to release Tom from the paper he had signed, and so he returned to Thetford with his father. Later that year he learned that the *Terrible* had foundered in a storm at sea and only twenty-five of her crew had survived.

For two more years Tom Paine stuck to the corset-maker's trade, but it seemed that almost day by day the drudgery of plying needle and thread grew more intolerable. He began to feel caged. And so he rebelled against his lot once again. England had declared war on France; the drumbeat of adventure quickened his pulse.

This time he sought a more distant port—Lynn— where his father couldn't catch up with him. He signed on as a member of the *King of Prussia's* crew. The ship was a privateer assigned to raiding French shipping.

In a very short time he learned that the warnings he had

been given about a sailor's life were all too true. Captain Mendez of the *King of Prussia* drove his crew to the limits of their endurance. Tom and his mates had to stand long watches, scramble up the masts in the roughest weather, live most of the time in wet clothing, and keep themselves going on the worst sort of food, hardtack and salt beef.

After a long cruise in the South Atlantic, however, the privateer failed to find any French ships and sailed back to London with her holds empty. The next time he boarded a ship, Tom swore, it would be as a passenger.

Yet he did not know what to do. At the age of twenty, he was a tall muscular youth with a ruddy face, dark intelligent eyes, and a long curving nose. His year at sea had given him a rugged frame. But he was equipped to do little except make corsets.

He hustled around the London streets trying to find a job, anything that would pay him a living and allow him to continue the studies begun in the Reverend Knowles's library—politics, literature, science, the physical world. He applied for work as a clerk in shops and law firms, as a porter at the Covent Garden market, as a government employee. Nobody would hire him. Finally, in despair, he turned back to the trade his father had taught him. A corset-maker in Hanover Street, Mr. Morris, as Tom wrote his parents back in Thetford, was willing to take him on as an apprentice. He would work at the trade during the day, attend geography and astronomy lectures at night at the Royal Society. The little time he had left was devoted to wandering through the back streets and lanes of London, where thousands of people lived in the grimmest poverty, many of them drunk day and night on penny-a-glass gin. The cheap gin was no temptation to Tom Paine. He saved his small wages from Mr. Morris' shop to buy a globe and secondhand books.

After a year's apprenticeship to Mr. Morris, he moved to Dover and worked for another corset-maker, then to Sandwich, a village in Kent, where he opened his own shop.

In Sandwich he met a young and pretty girl named Mary Lambert, who was an orphan and worked as a lady's maid. She was blonde and blue-eyed, and Paine fell in love with her. The only trouble was that his shop wasn't making enough money to support himself and a wife.

"I am not a businessman," Tom admitted to Mary when he asked her to marry him. "Probably I will never be able to dress you in silks, but I will do my best."

"Isn't that because your mind is not on corsets, but on all those books you read?" Mary asked with a smile.

"I hate corset-making," Tom replied, "I'd be a poor choice for a husband, I suppose. . . ."

"Most men would say that a servant and an orphan was not the best choice for a wife," Mary said. "We will have to make do with what we have."

Tom and Mary were married in the village church and she helped him in the shop which also served as their home. A few months later they moved to Margate, hoping business would be better there. Mary was going to have a baby. Again, however, Tom proved that he had little luck or talent for business. The shop took in so little money that he was unable to provide Mary with the nourishing food she needed, and she was frail besides.

Mary died in childbirth and their baby was born dead. When Tom buried the woman he loved and the child he wanted, he buried most of his youthful hopes.

No matter how hard he had worked he had been unable to support a wife properly. What kind of country was this, he wondered, that built an empire from India to America, yet could not or would not provide its citizens with decent homes and jobs? In the bitterness of his loss he became obsessed with the need for changing the world he knew. Meanwhile he needed a job to keep himself from starving. During his previous stay in London, he had been turned away from government offices on the grounds that he was too young. He was older now, and looked it. He would besiege the government until it found him a job.

A siege, as it turned out, wasn't necessary. The first government post for which he applied was that of exciseman—tax collector—and he passed the examination. The job paid him fifty pounds (about $250) a year, just enough to pay for his food, shelter, an occasional book.

For the next twelve years that was his work, making the rounds of shops and stores and taverns to make sure their owners had paid taxes on the goods they bought and sold. The work did not take much of his time, and he was able to continue the studies of politics, history, and philosophy which became the foundation of his career as a merciless critic of the government which now employed him. He also wrote many articles and essays which would be published in later years in America.

Most nights he spent debating the current political issues at the White Hart Tavern with the townspeople and working on essays no one would publish. Soon he was known as a man of fiery eloquence, a rather dangerous fellow who asked questions which any member of Parliament would have found difficult to answer. They centered on one issue: why did rich and powerful England treat her own people so poorly?

He lived over a tobacco shop kept by Samuel Ollive, who made snuff, cigars, and pipe tobacco in his workshop in the basement. Ollive had a wife and a daughter named Elizabeth, a pretty, blue-eyed, dark-haired girl some years younger than Tom.

To Elizabeth Ollive, Tom Paine seemed the most interesting and promising young man in that small Sussex town. What he needed to make a success of himself, she decided, was a wife. For that role she nominated herself, though she knew how tender Tom's memories of his first wife remained. Somehow, she decided, Tom would learn to love and forget the past.

Samuel Ollive died in 1771, leaving his widow and daughter only the house they lived in and his failing tobacco business. To Elizabeth this seemed the time for Tom Paine to be converted from lodger to breadwinner for the family. She suggested that, in addition to his tax-collecting post, he take over the tobacco business.

Only half seriously, he added to her suggestion: "And marry you, while I'm about it?" He saw that the suggestion was no joke to Elizabeth Ollive.

She glanced at him sharply, and said, "Why not?"

"I've always liked and admired you," Tom admitted. "You're a very pretty girl, and you have a firm character. You'd make an excellent wife for—"

"For you, Tom," she said quickly. "You need a wife to

[27]

steady you—all men do, but you especially. You wouldn't be wasting all your time talking, arguing, drinking at the White Hart. You'd have a wife and a business to concern yourself with."

"But, I don't think I'll fall in love more than once," Tom told her. "I loved Mary. There's . . ."

"I will *make* you learn to love me, too," Elizabeth said almost fiercely. "I'm a grown woman now, though you always seem to think of me as a young girl. You'll see, Tom. . . ."

It seemed the practical thing to do. Tom would take over the tobacco business and his friend Samuel Ollive's wife and daughter would be provided for. So he married Elizabeth and tried to provide more income for the family by adding groceries to the goods sold in the store. At the same time he continued with his tax-collecting job. Despite his hard work, however, the business did not prosper.

The year following his second marriage, 1772, he became involved in the first of many causes which were to make up his rebellious life.

All over England Paine and his fellow excisemen were angered by the government's refusal to pay them more than fifty pounds a year. Out of that had to come their expenses in traveling around the district in which they collected taxes.

Tom had become so well known for his eloquence that he was chosen to act as their spokesman. During the summer of 1772 he wrote a pamphlet titled *The Case of the Officers of Excise* and raised a fund of 500 pounds to present their case for higher pay to Parliament.

He spent the winter of 1772–73 in London, buttonholing members of Parliament and of the government to urge his cause. It was doomed to failure, but during that winter he met the man who was to change the course of his life —an American named Benjamin Franklin.

Benjamin Franklin had been discharged from his post as deputy postmaster general of the American colonies by the English government for protesting against "taxation without representation." Now he had come to London to urge the English government to reduce their taxes on the colonies. Paine had always been interested in science and he was fascinated by Franklin's experiments with electricity. Both men, too, were intensely interested in freeing men from the unjust burdens placed on them by governments.

At the time, of course, Franklin was older, wiser, and better known than Tom Paine, the obscure tax-collector from Sussex, afire with the cause of his fellow excisemen. To most of his fellow citizens, he was simply a troublemaker. Franklin, however, saw beneath that restlessness and divined a man of talent, someone he took seriously.

More than once, Franklin told him, "You should bend your thoughts toward America. We need men of your vigor and intellect, and your boldness in asking questions. What is there for you in England, beyond a thankless government job in which you have little hope of rising?"

Tom asked himself the same question, for neither Parliament nor the government would take action on his plea for fair treatment of the excisemen. There was nothing to do but return to Lewes, support his family, and keep the shop in Bull Lane going. In both efforts he failed. His employer, the Board of Excise, informed him that he was being fired for having spent so much time in London off the job.

At the same time the family tobacco shop ran into debt and a local court ruled that he would have to pay its debts or go to prison until they were paid. That was the law. He had no choice but to sell the contents of the shop at an auction.

Since he now was without a job, he told Elizabeth that he would have to go to London and look for work. He asked her if she wanted to accompany him. The marriage had not been a success, for he had not "learned to love" her as she had confidently expected, and because he was too pre-occupied with his "causes" to make good as a government employee or as a businessman.

Elizabeth decided to stay in Lewes with her mother, and told him, "Our marriage has failed because you are as poor a husband as you are a businessman."

He went back to London legally separated from his wife, thirty-seven years old now, and a failure in everything he had attempted. Occasionally he thought of Ben Franklin's suggestion that he go to America, but he did not have passage money. It was something to think about for the future.

For the present all his energies were focused on the next meal, the night's lodging. Finding only odd jobs to keep himself alive, he missed many meals, slept in the poorest of lodgings in the back lanes, and once again found that willingness to work counted for nothing. All that in the greatest city in the world, the capital of its most powerful nation, a city in which Charles James Fox, member of Parliament, lost 200,000 pounds (about $1,000,000) at the gambling tables one night while a citizen, Tom Paine, was trying to raise a few shillings for supper and a roof over his head.

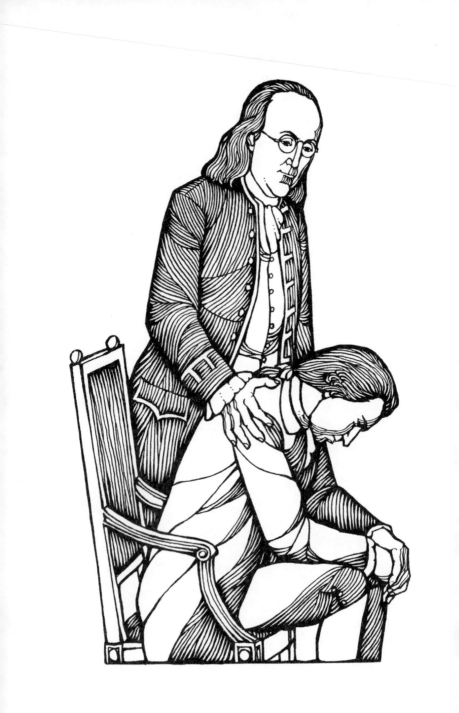

Passage to America

3

FRANKLIN'S ordinarily beaming face was shadowed with distress the moment he found Tom Paine on his doorstep, toward dusk one late-summer day in 1774.

"Are you ill, Tom?" Franklin anxiously inquired of his caller, whose clothes were torn and shabby, whose face was pale and gaunt from hunger. "Why haven't you come to see me?"

He guided Tom Paine into his sitting room, and before he allowed him to answer the questions he brought a loaf of bread, cheese, and a pitcher of beer.

"I've been too hard-pressed to see any of my friends," Tom explained as he wolfed down bread and cheese. "I'm at the end of my tether, no job, no home, and no prospects. I have come to you out of desperation. Ben, I must make a new start, I must get to America."

"Excellent!" Franklin replied. "The colonies need men like you, and will have greater need in the days to come. You should have come to me sooner, Tom. Meanwhile, I order you to finish every crumb of that food and every drop of that good English beer."

Tom needed no urging, and by the time he had finished his first solid meal in days his host was seated at the table working away with quill pen and ink at a letter of introduction.

"Take with you this letter to my son-in-law, Richard Bache of Philadelphia," Franklin explained, peering over at Paine through his small squarish spectacles. "He is a man of means and influence in that city, and will help you get started when you land there."

"When I land there?" Tom asked. "In Philadelphia? Why, sir, I haven't the money to pay my fare to Southampton!"

"Never mind that," Franklin told him. "I'll see to your passage." He cleared his throat and added, "This is what I've written my son-in-law: 'The bearer, Mr. Thomas Paine, is very well recommended to me as an ingenious, worthy young man. He goes to Pennsylvania with the view to settling there. I request you to give him your best advice and countenance, as he is quite a stranger there. If you can put him in the way of obtaining employment as a clerk or assistant tutor in a school, or assistant surveyor, of all of which I think him very capable, so that he may procure a subsistence at least, till he can make acquaintance and obtain a knowledge of the country, you will do well, and much oblige your affectionate father.' How's that?"

[34]

"I couldn't ask more of my own father," Tom said.

"You will repay me, and more, by spreading the ideas we have discussed in this room," Franklin replied. "My countrymen are sleepwalkers; they need an awakening. We require men in the colonies who are not afraid of speaking their minds, who are not afraid to throw down the gauntlet to the English Parliament, the English government, the English Crown itself. Oh, you'll be a good investment, Tom. Now let me tell you about Philadelphia. . . ."

In the last week of September, 1774, Tom Paine boarded the *London Packet* for the long dangerous crossing to America. Paine and three other passengers occupied the ship's small dark cabins. The accommodations were anything but luxurious. In Tom's cabin there was only a bunk and a washstand. It was no better than a cell, and recalled Samuel Johnson's remark that traveling by ship was worse than going to jail.

Yet Tom was one of the lucky few aboard the *London Packet*. Down in the hold of the ship were packed 120 men and women who were going to America as indentured servants. They were even poorer than Paine, who had the warm friendship of Ben Franklin. The indentured servant was practically a slave. He had to work for five or seven years for an employer who "bought" him in return for his passage to America.

The voyage across the North Atlantic, through autumn storms which buffeted the small sailing vessel, took nine weeks. As the ship rocked in the trough of great waves, Tom wondered more than once whether he'd ever see America. The seas were mountainous, the sky black and menacing most of the voyage.   He reflected that he'd been more comfortable as a member of the *King of Prussia's* crew than as a passenger aboard the *London Packet,* because the South Atlantic was calmer.

The food given the passengers in the steerage below was so poor that they were half starved.   They had little resistance when "putrid fever," probably typhoid, broke out below the decks.   Five of the indentured servants died and were buried at sea.

Tom himself caught the fever and lay in his bunk day after day, racked by pain and often delirious.   In his fever dreams, he was a boy back in Thetford, or was reliving the moment when his first wife and their stillborn child were buried in the churchyard, or was sailing again with Captain Mendez on the *King of Prussia.*

During the brief intervals when his mind cleared, he was certain that he would never reach America alive.

So, when the *London Packet* docked at Philadelphia on November 30, Tom was a living skeleton, so weak he could not leave his bunk.

One of the crew members, however, found the letter from Ben Franklin to his son-in-law among Tom's possessions.   He told several persons in the city about the letter from its best-loved citizen.   When a physician, Dr. Kearsley, heard of the letter, he drove in his carriage to the docks and boarded the *London Packet.*   Dr. Kearsley had the sick man carried off the ship, and took him to an inn on Market Street.

Under Dr. Kearsley's constant care, along with the nourishing food with which he was provided, Tom began throw-

ing off the effects of the fever.   It was three weeks, however, before he could leave his bed at the inn.   He had arrived in America close to death.   Now, with his health and
strength returning, he would make good on his promise to
Ben Franklin that he would help awaken the American
colonies to their destiny.

A Whiff of Revolution

4

WHEN HE WAS well enough to walk the streets, Tom Paine learned that, despite the tales sometimes told in England, America was not all a wilderness with a hostile Indian behind every tree. Philadelphia at the time of his arrival was a city of 35,000, the largest and wealthiest in the colonies. Many of the streets were paved for carriages and there were brick sidewalks. It was a cleaner and more prosperous city than many in England.

There was a brightness about the city that Paine had seen nowhere else. Many of the shopfronts were painted red, yellow, blue, or green, with large signs swinging out over the street and advertising their wares. Except for the Quakers, who dressed in drab colors, many of the Americans were clad in the height of colonial fashion. Men wore swords, cocked hats decorated with gold lace, silver buckles on their shoes. Many curled and powdered their hair. The ladies were even more elegant in silk, velvet, and brocade gowns, with hoop skirts so wide that they had to enter a door by turning sideways.

It was a sociable place, he discovered as he strolled past the London Coffee House on Front Street and the Indian Queen Hotel on Fourth Street. There members of the Continental Congress refreshed themselves between sessions over rum, brandy, wine, ale, and coffee.

There were poor people in Philadelphia, and New York City already had its slums, but poverty seemed to be less desperate here than in England. There were no ragged beggars. Even a poor laborer with a family lived in a decent enough cabin with plenty of ground around it on which to grow vegetables and fruit and keep a cow for milk.

In America there was an "openness," as Ben Franklin had said, but Paine noted immediately that there were two layers of society. There was a colonial aristocracy which aped the English. All others were lumped into a lower class, but they were not meek like the English, and there was great mobility out of that group. The American, no matter what his position, was a sturdy, independent, outspoken character who bowed his neck to no one. If a gentleman in a carriage splashed his stockings, he roared with rage and shook his fist. This tough sense of independence was what gave Tom Paine much hope for America and her future.

He took Franklin's letter of introduction to Richard Bache, who was married to Franklin's daughter Sarah and who was a wealthy importer.

Bache, after studying his father-in-law's letter, took

[*40*]

Paine to see a man named Robert Aitkin, who owned a bookstore and printing shop. After introducing the two men, Bache left them together in the printshop behind the bookstore.

Aitkin was a small, brown-eyed man with a cautious but friendly manner.

"So you're a writer, eh?" he asked Paine. "What I need is an editor. I have just begun publishing the *Pennsylvania Magazine,* and I need a man to take it in hand. If the magazine does not attract more readers, I will have to close it down. Are you the man for the job?"

Tom had never edited a paper of any kind, but he was more than ready to try.

"Yes," he replied, "if you are willing to give me a free hand and a living wage."

"Agreed," Aitkin replied. "I will pay you fifty pounds a year. If the magazine prospers, I will pay you more. Your own efforts will determine that."

They shook hands on the deal, and Paine settled down to his first career in the New World as editor of the *Pennsylvania Magazine.* He kept his room on Market Street and managed to live on one pound ($5) a week.

In its first few issues, the magazine showed the effects of Paine's intellectual vigor and outspoken opinions. In a few months he was able to write his sponsor, Ben Franklin, that Aitkin "had not more than 600 subscribers when I first assisted him. We now have upwards of 1,500 and daily increasing."

He had brought with him a number of essays and papers which he had written during the long restless years he lived in Lewes, Sussex, over the tobacco shop. Some of these were published in the *Pennsylvania Magazine* in addition to articles he wrote especially for it. It soon became evident to readers throughout the colonies that his was a fresh, unafraid voice willing to speak out on matters which most Americans discussed in whispers, and only with trusted friends.

There was more than a whiff of revolution in the air, but people were cautious about criticizing Mother England or the colonial government. Paine wasn't. He wrote of the state as a "necessary evil." He ridiculed the practice of settling disputes with dueling pistols, and denounced cruelty to animals, which few people thought wrong. He also declared that women should have rights equal to men.

Even more shocking to his readers was an article titled "African Slavery in America." Most Americans considered Negro slavery a part of the natural order of things, if they thought about it at all. Paine bluntly informed them that slavery was wrong in every way; in that he followed the doctrine of the Quakers. "Why do we here in America complain of attempts to enslave us," he demanded, "while we hold so many thousands in slavery?"

One morning in April 1775, about five months after he had arrived in America, Paine was aroused in his Market Street room by a tumult of shouting and cheering under his windows. A rider had just come galloping into the city with the news that Massachusetts Minutemen had fought a battle with the English troops at Concord and Lexington (April 19, 1775).

The Revolution had begun, in a sense, before the people were ready for it. Many had no real idea of what they

[*42*]

were fighting for, many others—the Tories—were opposed to throwing off British rule because they had prospered under it.

Later that morning, discussing the news with Richard Bache, Paine declared that he still considered himself a Quaker and therefore hated war, but "we must take a stand against the armed force of Britain."

First, however, the Americans must know why they were fighting the British army. In those first days after Lexington, Paine got the idea of writing down the principles upon which the colonies should take their stand against England. In a short volume, to be titled *Common Sense,* he would compress all his thought and feeling on the subjects of liberty and the right of the people to govern themselves.

With feverish concentration, he began writing nights after his work at Mr. Aitkin's shop on the *Pennsylvania Magazine* was done. He also attended meetings of the second session of the Continental Congress, convened in Philadelphia on May 10 to determine how the colonies would conduct their war for independence.

Ben Franklin had hastened back to America, arriving shortly after the Continental Congress began. At their first meeting, Franklin remarked, "You are an Englishman, Tom. It must be painful to take arms against your native country."

"I'm an American," Paine replied, his dark eyes flashing with anger at the suggestion that he still owed something to Mother England. "The King of England means no more to me than one of the dead Pharaohs of Egypt."

Franklin smiled and said, "The King may be able to ignore that, but some of his officials here are likely to take a

[*43*]

different view. Your writings are certain to provoke them, and you could count on a long term in prison if they lay hands on you."

"I'm a nimble fellow. I'll take my chances with the King's men."

During the rest of 1775 Paine worked on *Common Sense*, which he finished early in 1776 and took to a printer named Robert Bell. The pamphlet was to be sold for two shillings so it would reach a wide readership. Half the profits were to go to Bell and the other half to the Continental Army, of which George Washington had recently been appointed the commander.

It turned out to be the first best seller published in America and sold 100,000 copies in the first six months after publication. Paine's name did not appear on the title-page, but it was soon widely known that he was the author. Ideas from *Common Sense* were argued in coffee houses, Continental soldiers carried the pamphlet in their knapsacks. Washington wrote that it was "working a wonderful change in the minds of men." It was credited with providing inspiration for the Declaration of Independence a short time later.

Shortly after reading it, Ben Franklin asked Paine to come to his house for supper. "You've sounded the trumpet," Franklin told him. "The Revolution has its marching orders in this small book of yours. Sending you to America was the best day's work I've ever done."

Paine sipped his wine and smiled at his benefactor. "I don't feel that my work is finished with *Common Sense*. Suppose the Revolution succeeds. What then?"

"I think you can trust to the good faith and decency of

our leaders—Washington, Congress and all the rest—to see that we are justly governed."

"I trust no leaders," said Paine emphatically. "Power corrupts all men. We must protect ourselves against that corruption and there are other things to settle, even if we throw off the yoke of the English. Do we free ourselves and keep the Negroes in slavery?"

"A touchy matter," Franklin warned him.

"I believe in the freedom of man, wherever he is, whatever his color. That's the important thing."

"If you express yourself as vigorously as in *Common Sense*," Franklin said, "I shall not worry for the future of freedom on this continent."

He thumbed through a copy of *Common Sense* resting on the table, cleared his throat and read, " 'A government of our own is our natural right; and when a man seriously reflects on the precariousness of human affairs, he will become convinced that it is infinitely wiser and safer to form a constitution of our own in a cool, deliberate manner, while we have it in our power, than to trust such an interesting event to time and chance.' How true. And your words of warning against delay in seeking independence:

" 'Leaving the sword to our children,' you tell us, 'and shrinking back at a time when a little more, a little further, would have rendered this Continent the glory of the earth. . . .' "

Franklin turned the page and continued, " 'The sun never shone on a cause of greater worth. 'Tis not the affair of a city, a county, a province, or of a kingdom; but of a Continent—of at least one eighth part of the habitable globe. 'Tis not the concern of a day, a year, or an age; posterity are virtually involved in the contest, and will be more or less affected even to the end of time, by the proceedings now. Now is the seedtime of continental union, faith and honor. . . .'

"Glorious words," Franklin commented, "and the wonder is that they come from an Englishman. You have told us, with your clear vision, what we are and what we must become."

"Words, words," Paine said impatiently. "They won't win a revolution. Our country needs soldiers now. I think it is time that I dropped the pen and took up the sword."

"We can't spare you to the risks of battle," Franklin said. "There are many men brave enough to face the enemy, to march and fire a musket. Younger men than yourself are available to wear the uniform."

"I'm still a year less than forty," Paine protested, "and you are forgetting that in addition to those rousing phrases of mine you just quoted, I also wrote that the man who will not defend his country against the English oppressors has 'the heart of a coward and the spirit of a sycophant.' "

Before he kept that promise to join the Continental Army, Paine had to straighten out the dispute over the profits from *Common Sense* with Robert Bell, the printer.

"I wrote that pamphlet partly to provide funds for the army," Paine declared. "Now you tell me that profits don't exist. I'd like to know why, seeing that you're selling them as fast as your press can turn them out."

"But you insisted that they be sold for two shillings," Bell pointed out. "That barely pays the cost of printing and distributing, and the sellers take their share out first."

"Profits!" Paine snorted. "Don't any of you fair-weather patriots think of anything else? What do a few pence matter if the army is defeated for lack of supplies?"

He took the pamphlet out of Bell's hands and placed it with another printer. Adding an appendix and a special message for Quakers, he insisted that it be sold for one shilling instead of the two Bell had charged.

As it turned out, the second printer also claimed that no profits were coming in, again proving that Paine's many talents did not include one for business.

Thoroughly disgusted with people who cared more for money than their country, he went off to join the army. With him he carried very little—only an old knapsack and a water bottle.

With the Flying Camp

5

Tom Paine, recruit, left his lodgings on Market Street early one July morning in 1776, just a few days after the issuance of the Declaration of Independence, and walked down to the Mulberry Wharf.

Sixteen boats had been collected at the wharf to carry recruits from Maryland and Pennsylvania to the camps in New Jersey. Paine climbed into one of the boats just before it pushed off. It had been arranged that he should become the military secretary of General Roberdeau, who was an admirer of Paine's writings. A military secretary would now be called an adjutant.

Daniel Roberdeau, who operated a lead mine in western Pennsylvania to provide bullets for the Continental Army, commanded what was called the Flying Camp. It was an auxiliary force designed to move quickly to wherever it was needed most.

Late that day Paine and his comrades disembarked at Perth Amboy, New Jersey, which is about twenty miles below New York City and just across a narrow strip of water from Staten Island. The main British force under General Sir William Howe was then based on Staten Island.

When Paine arrived at General Roberdeau's headquarters to report for duty, he found the Flying Camp had just been set up. Everything was confusion. Some of the tents had not been erected, nor had most of the supplies arrived.

Paine strode up to Roberdeau just outside the headquarters tent. The general was a small, vigorous man about Paine's age, with sparkling blue eyes and a friendly manner.

When Paine introduced himself, Roberdeau exclaimed, "No one is more welcome in this camp! How we do need the common sense you write about, sir! I will trust to you to straighten out the housekeeping problem. Many of our troops are still on the road, so are the supplies, and we must get organized as soon as possible."

"I will do my best, General," Paine said, standing in what he hoped was a military posture, "though I must confess I am a rank amateur in an army camp."

"We're all amateurs, Paine! Having little or no experience, we must rely on common sense. And the military situation requires that this force place itself in readiness as quickly as possible."

"Bad news from General Washington?" Paine asked.

Lowering his voice and glancing around at the officers and men nearby, General Roberdeau said, "Come into my tent." Paine followed the general into the tent, which was occupied by a table on which maps were spread, a cot, and a leather chest. "The countryside is crawling with Tory spies," Roberdeau explained. "They have their ears to every keyhole, and not a few of them wear our uniform. Do you know the situation of General Washington's army?"

"Only the news published in the *Pennsylvania Magazine,*" Paine answered.

"Then I had better bring you up to date. The bulk of Washington's army is across the water, on Manhattan Island. The enemy is just across the way, on Staten Island. We expect that Howe will soon cross over to Manhattan and attack Washington." Roberdeau shook his head despairingly. "The outlook is very gloomy, my friend. Howe has at least 20,000 well-trained and well-fed regulars. Washington's forces include about 8,000 men, poorly armed, badly fed, and very close to despair. Granted the righteousness of our cause, what do you suppose the outcome of a clash would be?"

"Disaster," Paine said bluntly. "I have always said that Americans will fight bravely when the time comes, but they need something close to an even chance. One can't expect miracles."

"Exactly!" Roberdeau's forefinger traced the various positions on the map spread before him on the camp table. "Here we are at Perth Amboy, only a few hundred men, when they all arrive. Over there on Staten Island is Howe's sizable army. Obviously this force, the Flying Camp, could inflict no more than a pinprick on such a superior enemy. We are a post of observation at the moment. Our orders are to stay out of trouble, to report what we can see of Howe's movements—and *nothing*

[*51*]

more. Our only value to Washington is that we can provide him with news of Howe's movements against him. His only hope is that he will know just what the enemy is doing—understand?"

Paine nodded, but he did not try to conceal his feelings of disappointment.

"I hoped, sir," he said, "that we would be going into action against the English. That was why I joined the army —to fight, to risk my own life in a cause I have written so much about."

"You are worth more than an ounce of British lead," Roberdeau said firmly. "Concern yourself with your duties as my military secretary, and leave the bayonet work to strapping young farmers."

Paine busied himself around the Flying Camp through a hot and depressing summer. The force to which he was attached kept a close watch on the British over on Staten Island and sent word to Washington's headquarters when the enemy's ships began loading troops.

A few days later came bad news from the American forces on Manhattan. On August 27, 1776, the British attacked Washington's army, drove it out of Long Island, then out of Manhattan, and Washington was forced to retreat across the Hudson to New Jersey.

The Flying Camp broke up, its observation duties ended. Its men were transferred to Pennsylvania. That meant little action in the near future since the British and Americans would be confronting each other in New Jersey. Rather than accompany the Flying Camp away from the scene of action, Paine requested permission to attach himself to the headquarters of General Nathanael

Greene at Fort Lee, New Jersey, on the west bank of the Hudson opposite the northern end of Manhattan.

Paine was appointed General Greene's aide-de-camp, helping him in the planning and supplying of his division of infantry.

On November 20, as winter approached and a bitter wind blew down the Hudson, the British suddenly began crossing that river in force. Long lines of Redcoats climbed out of their boats and formed for the assault on Greene's camp. Cannonballs began falling in the camp and musket shots cracked out on both sides of the American breastworks.

Paine rushed from one end of the American position to the other, carrying orders from General Greene to his regimental commanders. Several times he was narrowly missed by musket balls. The Americans stood their ground for hours that day, but finally the British landed too many troops for them to handle.

"We're going to have to fall back," General Greene told Paine in the headquarters tent.

"Wouldn't it be better to hold out until night?" Paine suggested. "The men are worn out and they haven't been fed. If we waited until morning, sir—"

"I'd give anything if we could wait until the men were fed a hot meal," General Greene replied, "but we can't risk it. The British are beginning to move around our flanks. We might be cut off. Then the whole division would be gobbled up by the enemy."

"Yes, sir," Paine replied. "The Germans have a saying, 'Live today and fight another day.' "

He carried Greene's orders to the various regiments,

then waited with the rearguard as they began pulling out of the line and withdrawing from the breastworks they'd built around Fort Lee. A cold dismal rain was falling. The enemy's artillery increased its tempo, with cannonballs falling all around the retreating regiments.

Greene's rearguard doubled its rate of fire to make the enemy think the Americans were still holding their positions. Otherwise the British would have launched an all-out attack to prevent the Americans from escaping.

Then, slogging along with the rearguard over the muddy road, Paine himself was in retreat. Occasionally men fell from exhaustion or lack of food, but he noted that they always picked themselves up and rejoined the march. They were still fighting men, ready to turn on command and engage the enemy. Nor were the wounded abandoned to the enemy's mercy; their comrades carried them along on the retreat. Tents and other supplies had been left behind so that this was possible. After an all-night march, the division made good its escape to Newark.

With winter coming on, it appeared that the American cause was all but lost. Forced across the Delaware by unremitting enemy pressure, many thought the Revolutionary Army might not be able to survive until spring. During the early days of December, General Washington collected all available forces for a last effort to drive back the enemy. One resource he turned to was Tom Paine, for he believed Paine would be able to provide needed inspiration with his pen.

At Washington's request, General Greene brought Paine to see the commander-in-chief.

Gaunt with weariness, but tall and erect, Washington at their first meeting studied Paine in silence for a long moment. "So this is the man who gave us *Common Sense,"* Washington said finally, relaxing slightly. "General Greene tells me that you have worn the blue coat of a Continental soldier with honor. That places us doubly in your debt."

"If I had stayed in England," Paine replied, "if Mr. Franklin had not arranged for my passage to Philadelphia, I would still be scurrying around the back alleys of London in search of my next meal and night's lodging. The debt, sir, is on the other side."

"It's well that you feel that way about us," Washington remarked. He was pouring glasses of hot punch from a pitcher for himself, Paine, and Greene. "We have further use for your talents both as a soldier and a pamphleteer. First, however, I will ask you to give us a toast."

"My toast is always the same," Paine said, lifting his steaming glass. "To liberty."

Washington and Greene echoed the words, then Washington said, "I often read your articles in the *Pennsylvania Magazine.* We need something like that for the army. Let me explain. In a few weeks, God willing, I hope to launch an attack on the British and their German allies."

By "German allies," Washington meant the Hessians. They were troops from several German states literally sold to the British by their rulers. Not all came from Hesse, but they were generally known to Americans and British alike as Hessians.

"I intend," Washington continued, "to strike the enemy at his weakest point—the Hessians, for many of them have little love for the Union Jack. But first our own troops must know what they are fighting for, why they are here in the snow and cold while many of their fellow citizens toast themselves before their fires. Not everyone has read *Common Sense,* and besides conditions have changed. Our cause is not far from ruin. . . .

"Paine, I want you to begin printing your paper again. Tell the troops why so many sacrifices are required of them. Tell them if they fight now, the task will be easier, the assurance of eventual victory greater."

Paine, of course, agreed. He had joined the army to fight, but a man could fight with the pen when his comrades' morale needed boosting. Thus, in the snow-swept camp of Washington's army on the Delaware, he began writing the first issue of *Crisis,* a paper which he would publish from time to time whenever he had anything important to say.

Copies of his first *Crisis,* written on a drumhead beside a campfire, were distributed to the troops a few days before Washington made his supreme effort to cross the Delaware and show the British that Americans could fight hard and well under their own flag.

The very first paragraphs of that paper had a drumbeat that revived lost hopes and instilled a new determination in the army; they still ring so true they are often quoted almost 200 years later.

"These are the times that try men's souls. The summer soldier and the sunshine patriot will, in this crisis, shrink from the service of their country; but he that stands it *now* deserves the love and thanks of man and woman. Tyranny, like hell, is not easily conquered; yet we have this consolation with us, that the harder the conflict, the more glorious the triumph. . . ."

His words marched on: "What we obtain too cheap, we esteem too lightly; it is dearness only that gives everything its value.   Heaven knows how to put a proper price upon its goods; and it would be strange indeed if so celestial an article as FREEDOM should not be highly rated. . . . God Almighty will not give up a people to military destruction, or leave them to perish, who have so earnestly and so repeatedly sought to avoid the calamities of war by every decent method which wisdom could invent."

Everywhere the Revolutionary Army had been driven back during the past several months, but Paine told his comrades in arms, "I love the man who can smile in trouble, that can gather strength from distress, and grow brave by reflection. . . . I thank God that I fear not. . . . By persevereance and fortitude we have the prospect of a glorious issue. . . ."

That "glorious issue"—against all the odds—was soon forthcoming.   On Christmas Eve, 1776, Washington led his troops across the Delaware in rowboats to the eastern bank and the town of Trenton, which was garrisoned by Hessians.   Taken by surprise while celebrating, the Hessians were badly defeated.   Washington and his army moved on to Princeton, won another victory, and thus turned the tide.

The Revolutionary leaders credited Paine's flaming words in *Crisis* for a large share of the army's revived spirit, and even behind the battle lines, as a Philadelphia friend wrote him, "Your newest pamphlet has become the rallying cry of all Americans."

[57]

General Greene called him to headquarters one day early in January 1777, and revealed that there was need for another proclamation. Admiral Lord Richard Howe, he told Paine, had just issued an order commanding all Americans to lay down their arms and renounce the Revolution; otherwise "a terrible example" would be made of those who continued to resist the British armed forces. Since Admiral Howe was the brother of General Howe, the British commander-in-chief in America, his threats might be taken very seriously by the fainthearted.

"Address your next *Crisis* to Admiral Howe himself," General Greene suggested. "Make it plain that his threats will only strengthen our determination to stay in the fight. . . . I should warn you that the British are so angry with what you have written against them that General Howe says he can't make up his mind whom to hang first—you or General Washington."

Paine smiled and said, "I have never been given a greater honor." He remembered the Reverend Knowles warning him as a schoolboy against the dangers of not knowing his place. "An old teacher of mine said I ran the risk of ending up on the gallows."

In the middle of that month he published *Crisis No. II.* "By what means," he demanded of Admiral Howe, "do you expect to conquer America? If you could not effect it in the summer, when our army was less than yours, nor in the winter, when we had none, how are you to do it?"

The British generals, he continued, had been "outwitted" and their troops had been "outdone" in the recent battles, and "your advantages turn out to be your loss."

"I consider INDEPENDENCE as America's natural

right and interest," he wrote, "and never could see any real disservice it would be to Britain."

One day, he added, "the United States of America" would sound as important in the world as "the Kingdom of Great Britain."

Paine thus, in passing, created the title which the new nation would assume for itself. Until then no one had considered what Americans would call their country.

By the spring of 1777, with the army back on its feet, the Continental Congress decided that Paine's talents were needed in the Revolutionary government more than in the military camps. On April 17, it was proposed in Congress that Paine be appointed Secretary to the Committee of Foreign Affairs, which then functioned as an unofficial State Department. John Adams, future President, nominated him for the post, and General Roberdeau seconded him. He would be paid $70 a month—the most money he had ever earned.

As Secretary of the Committee of Foreign Affairs, Paine was something like a Secretary of State. He acted as middleman between the Congress and its agents in foreign capitals. In addition, whenever times were bad, he continued to bring out *Crisis* to revive and renew the spirit of liberty which made the Revolution live. Time and again, his fiery words of inspiration prevented the new nation from losing hope in its cause.

On September 11, 1777, General Washington and his army were badly defeated at Brandywine Creek and saved only by a quick night retreat. The British were marching on Philadelphia. A British fleet was coming up the Delaware River.

"Those who expect to reap the blessings of freedom must, like men, undergo the fatigues of supporting it," he wrote in *Crisis No. IV*. "We fight not to enslave, but to set a country free, and to make room upon the earth for honest men to live in."

For all his efforts, however, Paine made many enemies. There were those who envied his ability to influence the leaders of the Revolution. Some feared him because he was an honest man, others because he spoke out so fearlessly. Even after independence had been declared, at least a third of all Americans were said to be Tories, opposed to the war openly or secretly. The Tories hated Paine because they believed he was making a peace with the British impossible.

Those men, concerned more with their property and possessions than the hope of freeing the colonies, knew how to wait and strike when their enemy was weakest. They were waiting now for Paine.

The Silas Deane Affair

6

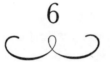

LATE IN 1777 and early 1778 the American Revolution seemed to be breathing its last. The British took Philadelphia, and the Continental Congress was forced to flee to Lancaster. That winter the American army suffered through the worst months of its history in the cold and mud of Valley Forge.

Paine often rode between Lancaster and Valley Forge, acting as a messenger between Washington and the Congress and observing the hardships of the army.

Having seen the soldiers suffering for lack of food and clothing and shelter made him all the angrier that an American could profit from the war. His anger, and the openness with which he expressed it, finally gave his enemies the chance to bring him down.

This happened at the climax of what became known as

the "Silas Deane Affair," which is still the subject of controversy among historians. It brought out all of Paine's rage for justice, all of his bitterness against those who were determined to profit from the war at the expense of the Revolutionary cause, but the question still lingers. Were Paine's suspicions entirely justified by the facts?

Silas Deane was sent by Congress to act as the American commercial agent in Paris. It would be one of his duties to obtain supplies from the French, even though France was not then in the war. French reluctance to help the Americans was increased by the fact they had a treaty with Britain they did not want to break openly.

The French, therefore, set up a private trading company under a colorful commoner named Beaumarchais, through which they would supply the Americans with gunpowder and other supplies needed to keep their armies in the field.

Silas Deane accordingly made deals with the private company headed by Beaumarchais, who later claimed—evidently with some truth—that he sold the supplies to the Americans at a loss to himself because he believed in their cause.

When the bills for these transactions came due, some members of Congress questioned them on the grounds that they were too high and insisted that Deane return to this country for an investigation. Hearings were held before the Congress, in which Deane was accused of having received money from the French for "personal expenses."

Tom Paine, predictably enough, was outraged by what he had heard of the "Silas Deane Affair." He condemned Deane not only for allegedly taking money from the French but on another score. It was charged that with no authority Deane had approached various German princes about coming to America to replace Washington as commander-in-chief.

Disregarding the fact that Deane was supported by some of the most powerful men in the Congress, Paine lashed out: "His [Deane's] whole life has been a fraud and his character is that of a plodding, plotting, cringing mercenary capable of any disguise that suited his purpose."

These were strong words, considering how few facts were then known, and Paine continued to attack Deane even after he was dismissed as commercial agent to Paris.

A friend of Paine's, who was one of the clerks of Congress and knew the forces against which Paine was setting himself, warned him against "hitting out too hard." The two men were having a glass of rum in a Lancaster tavern one night late in 1778.

"Deane could not have gotten away with tendering inflated bills if he didn't have influential friends in the Congress," the clerk said. "You have written a series of articles attacking him via *Common Sense,* and everyone knows that is the voice of Tom Paine. Your words strike not only at Deane but his friends. They won't let you get away with it."

"I'm striking at something rotten in the fabric of the Revolutionary government," Paine hotly replied. "No one but cowards would cheat the government while our troops were starving in Valley Forge and didn't even have shoes to wear. I have seen their bloody footprints in the snow! When I recall those footprints, I picture other men lining their pockets and dining with wine while the soldiers were getting a few handfuls of parched corn for their rations."

"True as that may be," his friend advised, "go easy for a bit. Just now France and America have worked out an alliance. Congress may have to disown you for the sake of that alliance if you don't halt your attacks on Deane and his friends. Think of your career. You may want to marry, raise a family here—"

Paine laughed harshly. "I've tried that," he said bitterly. "In business and in love I've always failed. That being the case I am married to my work—which right now is to see the country free of the English and safe from its own scoundrels."

His companion shook his head sadly, knowing it was all but impossible to swerve Paine from his chosen course. "Your work won't prosper if you make too many enemies. They say—"

"They say, they say!" Paine broke in. "I know what they say—that I hate women, that I don't believe in God, that I don't even have a proper respect for slavery as an institution. *They* also say I'm a drunkard and a manufacturer of libels. I know what they say, and I don't give a rap for the whole swivel-tongued lot of them!"

He would not be silenced. Under the signature *Common Sense,* he continued attacking Deane and his supporters.

"Who is Paine," demanded Gouverneur Morris, a leading financier of the American Revolution, "that he can tell his betters what is and what is not honest?"

His betters? That sneering remark, to Paine, was a

hateful echo of the English class system, which he hoped would not take root in America.

On January 6, 1779, he was summoned before a secret session of Congress and asked just one question:

"Are you the author of the articles signed *Common Sense?*"

"Yes."

Before he could say another word, he was told to withdraw from the chamber.

He knew then that certain members of Congress were determined to force him out of the secretaryship of the Committee of Foreign Affairs. That evening he sat down and wrote a letter to Congress:

"I cannot in duty to my character as a freeman submit to be censured unheard. I have evidence which I presume will justify me. . . . I entreat this House to consider how great their reproach will be should it be told that they passed sentence on me without hearing me. . . ."

Congress did not reply, but a few days later a friend of Paine's in that body passed the word that he was charged with having revealed in his writings passages from certain documents concerning the supply deals with the French, which he had read as Secretary to the Committee on Foreign Affairs.

On January 9, he sent his resignation to Congress and declared, "I have revealed no secrets because I have told nothing that was, or I conceive ought to be, a secret."

Paine had made himself a dangerous man, not only because he attacked what he considered dishonesty but because he proclaimed himself the judge of what should be kept secret. The French government leaders, at least, recognized his ability as a pamphleteer and wanted to make sure they wouldn't be the target of his wrath. Only a few days after he resigned they offered him $1000 a year if he would write favorably about the French alliance, but Paine declined.

Mission to France

7

GOUVERNEUR MORRIS called Paine "a mere adventurer from England, without fortune, without family or connections." He was right about Paine's lack of fortune, family, and connections, but he was wrong if he thought that some of the bravest and most intelligent men of the Revolution —many of them fighting under Washington's banners— were not his supporters. They could not rally around Paine and save his job, or defend him in secret sessions of Congress, but they believed in the author of *Common Sense* and the *Crisis* papers.

Among those who counted themselves as supporters of Tom Paine were three future Presidents—Thomas Jefferson, James Madison, and James Monroe; Benjamin Franklin, then representing Congress in France; Generals Roberdeau and Greene; and Henry Laurens, a former president of Congress.

After losing his job as Secretary of Foreign Affairs, Paine was hard-pressed to keep himself in food and shelter for a time. All the money he could spare from his salary, all his earnings from his pamphlets had been donated to the Revolutionary treasury. Then his friends in Pennsylvania found him a post. He was elected clerk of the Pennsylvania Assembly, then the equivalent of a state legislature.

One of his first duties, in November of 1779, was to write part of Pennsylvania's law abolishing slavery, which freed 6,000 Negroes from bondage. Several months later the University of Pennsylvania honored him with a Master of Arts degree. If there is an art of propaganda, he was certainly its master.

About that time the American forces were suffering a disaster in the southern theater of the war. Charleston, South Carolina, and Savannah, Georgia, had been captured by the British army. Meanwhile Washington's army, camped around White Plains, was merely "watching" the British occupation force in New York City. Washington, in fact, didn't dare take the field. His troops were close to mutiny because they hadn't been paid and they lacked food and other supplies.

To relieve that situation, Paine started a fund for Washington's soldiers with $500 he had scraped together. Soon it amounted to more than a million dollars as others contributed. Washington's army was provisioned, and the mutiny subsided—thanks to Paine's quick action.

Later that year, 1780, he wrote a *Crisis* paper on the subject of taxation. Americans hated taxes, he observed, the Stamp Act being one of the causes of the Revolution, but taxation was necessary if the fight against the English was to be continued.   Otherwise the soldiers wouldn't be paid, fed, or clothed, and the Revolutionary government might collapse.   The paper money issued by the government was almost without value, and had become a bad joke.   Nevertheless Congress decided against taxation, and decided instead to ask France for an $8 million loan.

Colonel John Laurens was appointed to make the plea for a loan, and Paine was asked to accompany him as advisor.   (Laurens was the son of Henry Laurens, former president of Congress and a firm supporter of Paine's).   For such a delicate piece of diplomacy, Paine was a curious choice.   He had shown no talent for diplomacy, and he was not in high favor with the French because of the Silas Deane Affair.   Yet Paine was determined to show that he could not only attack, but could reconcile; that he could loyally carry out the government's policy, even though he favored taxation over a loan from the French. It was his chance to regain a position in which he could be influential.

Young Colonel Laurens told him, "I will accept the appointment only if you come with me.   My only experience has been military, I know nothing of politics or finance. What can I say to persuade you?"

Paine smiled and said, "Nothing.   I don't need any persuasion.   Ben Franklin is in Paris with the American commission, and I haven't seen him for several years.   As for your mission, we'll be glad to advise you on the political and financial side.   The French generals will have a lot of questions, too, and they'll be your job."

They boarded the frigate *Alliance* at Boston on February 11, 1781.   She was a swift, well-armed ship.   The

North Atlantic was full of British naval vessels blockading the American ports and trying to cut off all commerce, and it was hoped that the *Alliance* could outrun or outfight any enemy warship that tried to intercept her. Paine knew that if he was captured by the British he would be taken to the Tower of London and executed.

The *Alliance,* however, arrived safely at the French port of Lorient. Several days after their arrival on March 9, Paine was reunited with Benjamin Franklin in Paris.

It soon became apparent that Congress had made a mistake in choosing young Colonel Laurens for any diplomatic post. He was twenty-six years old, hot-tempered and arrogant. As a member of the South Carolina aristocracy, he had always had his own way. It was hard for Paine and Franklin to convince him that the French must be persuaded, not commanded.

Laurens got along all right with the French generals, who wanted to know just how much strength and spirit was left in the American army after almost six years of fighting. He convinced them that there was plenty of fight left in the Revolutionary soldier. But it was a different matter when he called on Vergennes, the crafty old foreign minister of France. Vergennes wanted facts and figures. France was not about to sink $8 million in a losing cause, even though by now a French army had landed in America.

After his first interview with Vergennes, Paine and Franklin had a long talk with the hotheaded young Colonel Laurens. They had heard that the foreign minister was displeased by what Laurens told him.

"Just what did you tell Vergennes?" Franklin asked.

[*74*]

"The truth, sir," Laurens snapped. "The straight and simple truth. That we cannot proceed without money and supplies. That the French army has been idling, and if it will not fight at least the French can supply men who *will* fight. That Washington and his army cannot stay in the field without that help."

"Strong medicine," Paine commented. "The French are not accustomed to being talked to that way."

"And you are a very young man," Franklin gently reminded Laurens, "addressing a man old enough to be your grandfather. I received word from the foreign ministry that Vergennes will not receive you again unless you promise to mend your manners."

"I don't care a fig for manners," said Laurens hotly.

"But the French do," Franklin murmured. "What else did you tell Vergennes?"

"I said that if we weren't given help," Laurens answered, a little less boldly, "that we would have to pull out of the war. Then we would join England in its war against France."

Paine groaned and said, "It will be a miracle if we aren't deported from France. Look, Henry, you've got to remember that we're playing the beggar's role here."

"I won't beg," Laurens declared. "We're asking little enough, considering all we've sacrificed and considering how much France has to gain from defeating England."

"Patience, patience," Franklin sighed. "Paine, tell this young Hotspur that nations never speak plainly to each other. The same goes for diplomats. The quickest way to lose out with the French is to lose your temper. They're

[75]

experts at baiting us. They will push us into a position in which we would have to accept whatever they feel like giving."

Paine took Laurens aside and persuaded him that, for the sake of the American cause, he must send an apology to Vergennes. Paine himself was received by the King and various high officials of the government, and managed to smooth matters over. Franklin also worked his great charm on members of the French government; undoubtedly his great prestige among the French was more important than Paine's work in the final result.

Thus when Paine and Laurens sailed back to America August 25, 1871, they brought with them the resources the colonies needed in the final stage of the war. The French frigate *La Résolute* not only carried Paine and Laurens back to America in style, but its holds were loaded with 2,500,000 louvres, silver money, packed in casks. Two other ships loaded with supplies accompanied her. Another 7,500,000 louvres—the balance of the $8 million loan—would be sent shortly. In addition the French were making an outright gift of 6 million louvres.

Paine and Laurens, with their cargo of silver, were joyfully welcomed when they landed on the wharves of Boston. The casks filled with silver coins were loaded into sixteen oxcarts. Following them were other carts carrying the gunpowder and other military supplies—a long procession that rolled slowly down the roads from Boston to Philadelphia.

Along the way people in all the towns and villages turned out to cheer the procession. The means of victory were passing them in review.

Within a few weeks Washington's army was paid, clothed and fed—thanks to the loan and gift Paine was in large part responsible for obtaining. The American army closed in on the British under Lord Cornwallis at Yorktown, Virginia. With them, on land and sea, moved the French. Cornwallis was trapped in his elaborate fortifications and on October 19, 1781, he and his 7,000 troops surrendered. It was not the end of the war, but the British could no longer hope for victory.

Rewards of Victory

8

For almost two more years the British insisted on maintaining a state of war with the American colonies, though the war had effectively ended with the British defeat at Yorktown. Until a peace treaty was signed in 1783, the British refused to admit they had lost and obviously hoped their former subjects would start fighting among themselves. It was a dangerous period for the new nation.

George Washington recognized that the spirit and morale of the American people had to be kept at the pitch which had brought them so close to freedom. The one man who could inspire them, make them see their duty, was Tom Paine.

Despite all he had done for the cause, Paine was jobless and all but penniless. For a time he supported himself as a Philadelphia merchant's clerk. But early in 1782 he had no means of support. The man who a few months earlier had helped arrange an $8 million loan from the French could not persuade his government to find him a job. So he appealed to General Washington, who had always recognized the value of Paine's efforts.

Twice Washington wrote the officials of the government in Philadelphia asking that Paine be given a job. They ignored Washington's requests. Finally, on January 26, 1782, Washington journeyed from the headquarters of his army in Virginia to Philadelphia and called Robert Morris, the Superintendent of Finance, and Robert Livingston, who now held Paine's old post of Secretary of Foreign Affairs, into a meeting.

"Paine," Washington told Morris and Livingston, "must be given a decent job with the government."

"Naturally," Morris said, "we are grateful to Mr. Paine for his services, but the treasury—"

"Gratitude has nothing to do with the case," Washington curtly interrupted. "We need his help as much as he needs ours. Disunity is still a threat, the Tories and the British haven't given up. Paine's pen is our best weapon against them."

"Congress would never approve of placing him in the government again," Livingston declared. "Those *Common Sense* articles of his are still bitterly remembered by their victims."

Washington shook his head. "If I ask for a new division of fighting men, you do your best to raise them. Paine is worth a division by himself. I think that if you gentlemen will just puzzle your wits for a moment you will find a way of employing Mr. Paine without bringing the government down around our ears."

There was a long silence in the room.

Finally, Morris, who in effect was the Secretary of the Treasury, cleared his throat and announced, "He could be paid out of the Secret Service Fund, for which we do not have to account to Congress."

Paine, it was thus arranged, would draw a salary of $800 from the government while resuming the writing and publishing of the *Crisis* papers.   For those invaluable services he had to be paid secretly.   This was chiefly because of the enmity of Silas Deane's supporters.   Paine had never been forgiven for his part in the Silas Deane Affair.   After the war it was revealed that Deane had written letters to friends in America from Europe saying that the colonies should have stayed with the British Empire and that the leaders of the Revolution were evil men.   Primarily because of Deane's role in arranging the French Alliance along with Ben Franklin, his estate was later voted $37,000 by Congress, but his collaborator Beaumarchais struggled unsuccessfully for years to be repaid by the French government or the United States government.

With his usual enthusiasm, Paine returned to the task of keeping his fellow Americans alert to the dangers of growing slack before the war was won.   In one issue of *Crisis* he warned: "Perhaps one of the greatest dangers which any country can be exposed to, arises from a kind of trifling which steals upon the mind when it supposes the danger past; and this unsafe situation marks at this time the peculiar crisis of America."

In another issue he pointed out: "The policy of Britain has ever been to divide America in some way or other.   In

[*81*]

the beginning she practiced every art to prevent or destroy the union of the states. . . . Failing in this project in America, she renewed it in Europe; and, after the alliance had taken place, she made secret offers to France to induce her to give up America. . . ." The British, he warned, would keep trying to divide the Americans and encourage them to fight among themselves until the last British flag had been hauled down and the last British soldier left the soil.

The British finally decided to sign a peace treaty in 1783, because fighting the Americans was costing them too much and they had failed to disunite the states. In April 1783, Paine issued his last *Crisis* paper, almost seven years after he had published the first during the dark December days preceding the victory at Trenton. "The times that tried men's souls are over, and the greatest and completest revolution the world ever knew, gloriously and happily accomplished." But now, he added, America would have to meet new tests. She would have to show the world that she could "bear prosperity" and that "her honest virtue in time of peace is equal to the bravest virtue in time of war."

No country, he said, ever had greater opportunities than this one to "make a world happy—to teach mankind the art of being so. . . ."

With that his long series of pamphlets ended, and Paine retired to the New Jersey countryside to seek the joys of private life.

From his savings as a "secret" employee of the Revolutionary government, he was able to buy a small house near the village of Bordentown, New Jersey, on the Delaware River about 35 miles from Philadelphia. Nearby was the home of an old friend, Colonel Joseph Kirkbride, who was about Paine's age. Paine was forty-six years old when the Revolution ended. It was cheaper living in the village than in a city like Philadelphia, a matter of some importance because Paine had only a small income from his writings.

Meanwhile General Washington and his wife had taken a house at Rocky Hill, near Princeton. Washington had not yet been elected the first President of the United States, but he was keeping in close touch with Congress, which was still meeting in Philadelphia.

Washington was concerned, as he wrote Paine, because Congress had not found a way to reward Paine for his services. In the fall of 1783, he wrote Paine inviting him to visit the Washington home at Rocky Hill. "Your presence might remind Congress of your past services to this country," Washington said in the letter, adding that he would do anything he could to help in that cause.

Paine did go to visit the Washingtons, was warmly received by the General, and treated to weeks of Virginia hospitality. Congress took note of the visit, as Washington had expected. It finally recognized at least part of the nation's debt by awarding Paine $3,000 in cash. Subsequently the Pennsylvania Assembly voted him $2,500 and the State of New York gave him a house and a 277-acre farm near New Rochelle.

He was financially secure for the first time in his life, and began to receive some of the honors to which he was entitled. The next several years, in fact, were probably the happiest and most carefree of his life. After a visit to the farm at New Rochelle given him by the State of New York, he decided that he would continue to make the place at Bordentown his headquarters.

Perhaps he preferred to live there because it was closer to Philadelphia, to which Ben Franklin had recently returned from France. Paine often rode into the city to talk with his old friend. Franklin called him "my adopted political son." They still held in common a love of scientific subjects, particularly inventions.

With politics temporarily not his main concern, Paine busied himself with a number of inventions. One was a smokeless candle, which Franklin encouraged him to develop. Both men, while laboring at their writings and studies, suffered from the smoke of tallow candles which irritated their eyes. Paine invented a smokeless one with three holes running parallel to the wick. Supposedly it eliminated the tallow smoke. He persuaded a candle-maker to adopt his design, but it was never a success.

Congress met in New York in 1785, and Paine then made a number of trips to that city. He attended balls and dinners at which young people gathered around him. Many were too young to have fought in the Revolution, but they had read *Common Sense, Crisis* papers, and other writings. It was natural enough that he appealed to youth.

In all his works, he refused to accept any ideas merely because they were old and traditional. He insisted that *man* was more important than *property,* that the world could be made a better place if people were willing to discard the past. To young nations and young people, Tom Paine would always be a hero.

Inspiration from a Spider

9

DURING THE several years following the Revolution, Paine spent much of his time in the lean-to which served as a workshop behind his house at Bordentown.   "For the first time in my life," as he wrote a friend, "I have the leisure and the money to carry out my scientific ideas."

One of those ideas was for the construction of a bridge built entirely out of iron.   Until now, all bridges in America were made of wood, and they didn't last long because their wooden supports rotted in the water.

One day his friend and neighbor Colonel Kirkbride entered the shed and found Paine intently studying a spider building his web in a corner near the workbench.

"There," said Paine approvingly, "is nature's finest engineer."

"The spider an engineer?" the puzzled Kirkbride asked. "What are you talking about, Tom?"

[87]

"Look at his web," Paine enthused. "Its strands are fine as silk and yet it will support objects many times its weight. Why? Because of the artfulness of its construction. That spider, in fact, has given me an idea of how an iron bridge should be constructed.

"Have you ever seen a European bridge?" he continued. "It's made of arches resting in mid-river on a pier. That won't do for North America, because of the great amounts of ice in our rivers. The ice breaking up in the spring would damage the pier.

"Now my iron bridge will arch over the river in one swoop, without support from a pier in mid-river. It will be strong enough to eliminate the need for a pier. By heaven, Kirkbride, I'll make my fortune yet—thanks to the spider!"

For months he labored in his workshop building models of his bridge, the first of wood, the second of cast iron, the third of wrought iron. He was assisted in this work by John Hall, a middle-aged English mechanic who had migrated recently to America. It was interrupted only when various visitors came to call, such as Benjamin Franklin, Dr. Benjamin Rush, Robert Morris, and other associates of the Revolutionary years.

Franklin, as a fellow inventor, was enthusiastic about Paine's scheme when he examined the cast-iron model in the workshop at Bordentown one day.

"You must put it to practical use as soon as possible," he told Paine.

"I intend to do just that," Paine said. "See that wooden model in the corner over there? It's thirteen feet long and built to scale. I'm going to take it on a sled to Philadelphia in a few weeks and show it to a committee of the Pennsylvania Assembly. I'm hoping they will be convinced an iron bridge could be thrown across the Schuylkill River near Philadelphia."

"But the Schuylkill is 400 feet wide," Franklin said. "It can only be crossed by ferry at the moment. No one has dared think of bridging it. How can you be sure your bridge wouldn't sag right into the water?"

"Look," Paine replied, bending down to point out features of the wooden model on the floor. "These iron girders are put together in crisscross fashion, like a spider's web. They will distribute the weight to the piers at each end of the bridge. The stress will be on the structure as a whole rather than at any particular point."

"But the amount of iron it would take—" Franklin protested.

"More than 500 tons, I calculate," Paine admitted. "Our few iron-smelters would be hard pressed to fill such an order. Good! It will cause an expansion in our iron industry."

Shortly before Christmas, 1786, Paine hauled the thirteen-foot wooden model of his bridge to Philadelphia for inspection by the Pennsylvania Assembly's committee. But first he placed it on exhibition in the garden of Ben Franklin's house on Market Street. Hundreds of people came to see it. Paine invited those interested to walk on the bridge, stamp hard on it, to show that it would hold their weight without cracking.

It was considered something of a marvel, and the Assembly committee agreed that it might be workable. The only question in their minds was whether it would be equally practical in a full-scale 400-foot shape. Nothing like it had ever been tried. The committee informed Paine that it would have to study the matter.

That study went on month after month, and Paine was not a patient man. Late in April 1787, he decided to take the model of his bridge to France and have it studied by the Academy of Sciences. He might also show it to the Royal Society in London, where he had attended lectures so many years ago. If the best scientific brains in France and England approved of his project, it might influence the Pennsylvania Assembly.

He was given a fine welcome in Paris, particularly by his old friend Thomas Jefferson, who was American minister to the court of King Louis XVI, and the Marquis de La Fayette, who had fought hard for the American Revolution.

Jefferson was greatly interested in Paine's bridge. He introduced Paine to the officials of the Academy of Sciences, which appointed a committee of three men to study the thirteen-foot model of the bridge which Paine had brought with him.

One day late in August 1787, only a few months after he arrived in Paris, Paine was shown to the study at Jefferson's home.

Jefferson looked up from the papers on his desk and remarked, "Either you're in a great state of excitement, Paine, or August in Paris is too much for you. I thought you'd be spending the month in the country like most sensible people."

"Commune with the cows and horses when I was waiting for word from the Academy's committee?" Paine snorted.

"I should say not! Well, Jefferson, the committee has tendered its report."

"Good or bad?"

"Good!" Paine removed a sheaf of paper from the pocket in his coattail. "Listen to this, my friend. The committee says my bridge is 'ingeniously imagined.' It goes on to say that judging from the model it is 'simple, solid, and proper to give it the necessary strength for resisting the effects resulting from its burden.' The committee notes that until now, in France, iron has been used mostly for making weapons, pots and pans, nails, the rims of wagon wheels, but it is time they started thinking about wider uses for the metal—such as my bridge!"

"Excellent," the red-haired Jefferson murmured, "excellent. Now what will you do?"

"Take the model to England and show it to the Royal Society. I also intend to visit my native village of Thetford. My mother is ninety years old and I haven't seen her since leaving England many years ago."

A few days later he left for London, where he took the wooden model of his bridge to Sir Joseph Banks, president of the Royal Society, who promised to give an opinion on its usefulness. Otherwise he was not officially received in London, because he had publicly turned against his native land to fight for the rebellious colonies. Few had read *Common Sense* at the time because its publication, naturally enough, was forbidden in England.

He paid a visit to Thetford, where the older people remembered him as a young rascal who had run away to sea, had got into a number of scrapes and gone to America and fought against King and Country. The people of Thetford had always thought he'd come to no good, and their opinion was not changed by reports that Tom had become a scribbler and harebrained inventor of some notoriety.

His aged mother was gladdened by his visit and his promise that he would continue to provide for her. His father had died in the past year from the smallpox.

Thetford had not changed in all the years he had been away. To him it was even more drab and narrow-minded than it had been. With some relief, he soon left his native town for London. There was good news awaiting him from Sir Joseph Banks. The latter said he believed Paine's bridge was practical and considered it a "work of genius."

For almost a year Paine was occupied with plans for building a large model of his iron bridge. An American merchant living in England, Peter Whiteside, became interested in the project. Whiteside agreed to put up the money to have a 110-foot iron bridge built at the Walker Iron Works in Rotherham, Yorkshire, and in 1788 Paine took out English patents on his invention.

Paine then went to Rotherham to supervise construction of the bridge at the iron works. From Rotherham he wrote Thomas Jefferson in Paris: "The Walkers are to find all the materials, and fit and frame them ready for erecting, put them on board a vessel and send them to London. . . . We intend first to exhibit it and afterwards put it up for sale, or dispose of it by private contract. . . . My principal object in this plan is to open the way for a Bridge over the Thames. . . ."

Once the bridge was built it was set up in a London park, Paddington Green, where people paid one shilling (about twenty-five cents) to walk across it. Thousands paid their shilling, for an iron bridge 110 feet long was then a great curiosity—the only one of its kind. Some years later a 236-foot bridge built according to Paine's patented design was used to span the River Wear in England. It was never accepted, however, by the Pennsylvania Assembly to bridge the Schuylkill.

During those two or more years in England, Paine found himself accepted, gradually, by the political leaders and other influential men of England. He spent a weekend with Edmund Burke, who had argued for American freedom in Parliament; he was on friendly terms with the Duke of Portland, the head of the Whig party; the Marquis of Lansdowne; Charles James Fox; and Sir George Staunton. They called him, only half-jokingly, the "unofficial American ambassador."

Partly as a sign of his acceptance, his portrait was being painted by the famous George Romney. An old friend named Thomas Clio Rickman, once a fellow exciseman, described Paine as he sat for the Romney portrait. Paine at the age of fifty-two was an impressive figure with brilliant and piercing eyes, Rickman noted. "In his dress and person, he was generally very cleanly, and he wore his hair queued, with side curls, and powdered, so that he looked altogether like a gentleman of the old French school. His manners were easy and gracious; his knowledge was universal and boundless; in private company and among his friends, his conversation had every fascination that anecdote, novelty, and truth give it."

Paine soon learned that the purpose of some of the British political leaders was to flatter him into falling in with their schemes for recovering the American colonies. He wrote Jefferson in March 1789 that he was no longer being courted by the Marquis of Lansdowne because of "my coldness and reserve" on the subject of reuniting England with America.

The English establishment would soon have a much better reason for detesting Tom Paine and all he stood for.

On July 14, 1789, the second revolution that was to change the political history of the world took place. Partly under the inspiration of the American uprising, the people of France revolted against King Louis XVI, the nobles, and upper classes. July 14—Bastille Day—was the day when the people of Paris broke down the doors of the prison that symbolized their oppression.

Paine, of course, knew many of the revolutionaries in Paris, among them La Fayette, and he wanted to see for himself what was happening in France.

Later in the year he journeyed to Paris and was warmly welcomed by La Fayette and the others. The young Marquis, who had turned against his own class in his determination to see his country freed of the immense burden of its wasteful monarchy, had acquired the large iron key to the Bastille shortly after that prison was captured.

"I want you to give this key to General Washington," La Fayette told Paine. "It is fitting that you should receive the key first, because you inspired the American Revolution. It is fitting that Washington should be given the key, finally, because he made a success of the struggle in America."

[*94*]

Paine at first intended to present the Bastille key to Washington in person, but he found that the business of promoting his iron bridge would keep him in England for a year or more. So Paine sent it to Washington, now President of the United States, with a letter reading:

"I feel myself happy in being the person through whom the Marquis has conveyed this early trophy of the spoils of despotism, and the first ripe fruits of American principles transplanted into Europe, to the great master and patron. . . . That the principles of America opened the Bastille is not to be doubted, and therefore the key comes to the right place."

On his return to England after meeting with the leaders of the first phase of the French Revolution, Paine soon found himself plunged into controversy. His career as a rebel, as an arouser of the public conscience, as a molder of opinion, was not over. No doubt he welcomed the opportunity to return to the arena. A good fight made life worth living.

Edmund Burke, whom Paine had considered a friend and fellow believer in progress, had just published a pamphlet titled *Reflections on the Revolution in France*. Paine was surprised by the fact that Burke upheld "the divine right of kings," called the people of France a "violent rabble," and declared that the French Revolution was a menace to civilization. Yet this was the man who had defended the American colonists when they threw off British rule! What had caused the change in Burke? Neither Paine nor any of his other associates knew it, but for several years Burke had been in the service of the British Crown.

He was being paid 1,500 pounds a year from King George's private funds to uphold the monarchy as a writer and orator.

Paine didn't know what had caused the change in Edmund Burke, but he decided immediately that Burke must be answered.

He settled down in an inn at Islington, a quiet London suburb, to write the book he titled *Rights of Man.* It was not merely a reply to Burke but a defense of man's right to live in freedom and not be oppressed by his government. What *Common Sense* was to the American Revolution, *Rights of Man* was to be to men everywhere. It also advocated an international organization like today's United Nations, which was to do away with conflicts between nations. Much of what he wrote is widely accepted now, but 180 years ago it was a revolutionary document in every sense of the word. It told people that their rulers had not, as they claimed, been chosen by God; that they had a right to govern themselves.

The difference between him and Burke, as Paine saw it in *Rights of Man,* was that "I am contending for the right of the *living,* and against their being willed away, and controlled and contracted for, by the manuscript-assumed authority of the dead; and Mr. Burke is contending for the authority of the dead over the rights and freedom of the living." It was wrong, he wrote, that kings should "consign the people, like beasts of the field, to whatever successor they appointed."

He emphasized that "Man has no property in man; neither has any generation a property in the generations which are to follow."

He struck hard at the belief that only those who owned property had a right to vote and share in the control of their government.

Rights of Man caused a great stir when it was published early in 1791, not only in England but in America. In the United States it supported the views of Jefferson and Madison that the United States should be a truly democratic Republic and opposed those of such men as John Adams and Gouverneur Morris, who believed that Americans should be divided into upper and lower classes, that the American system should closely resemble the British, and suggested that the office of President should be made hereditary. Adams, who was to be the second President, once credited Paine with being the chief mover of the Revolution, but now he considered him to be nothing more than a disturber of the peace. But Thomas Jefferson, now Secretary of State, saw to it that *Rights of Man* was published in the United States. Jefferson wrote the printer that it would counteract the "political heresies which have sprung up among us. . . . I have no doubt our citizens will rally a second time round the standard of *Common Sense.*"

In England *Rights of Man* caused a political earthquake. Paine was denounced as a dangerous radical. If he favored the overthrow of the French monarchy, and the people agreed with him, what would happen to the throne of Great Britain?

Agents of King George tried to buy up all copies so they would not reach the people. Paine himself was denounced in newspapers and pamphlets. His effigy—a scarecrow made of straw and paper—was burned on many occasions and his name was blackened at public meetings.

There were rumors that hirelings of the throne had been promised a large reward if they succeeded in killing Paine.

His friends begged him to flee the country before he was mobbed or assassinated.

"I will not run," he always replied to their appeals.

The threat of violence hovered over Paine even as the English public read the *Rights of Man,* many with secret approval. More than 200,000 copies were sold in England alone. Finally the government ruled that it was "seditious" and no more copies could be sold.

One night in the summer of 1792 Paine attended a party in London at which William Blake, the poet, was also a guest. Blake had learned earlier that evening that the Home Office had issued orders that Paine be arrested and all his papers seized. He would probably be placed on trial for his life.

Blake took him aside at the party and whispered, "You must not go home. If you do, you will be going to your death."

Paine believed him. He did not go home, but slipped out of London that night, went to Dover and boarded a ship for France.

The Cross of Death

10

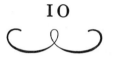

Warmly welcomed by La Fayette and other friends, Paine settled down in Paris to help the French people establish a Republic. He soon learned that he would never be able to return to England. Even though absent, he was tried before the King's Bench in Guildhall and found guilty of high treason. If he ever returned to England or set foot on any of her possessions, he would be hanged.

In France, as earlier in America, Paine made himself at home. His *Rights of Man* was published in a French translation and immediately made him one of the heroes of the French Revolution. He was made a citizen of France and elected to the National Convention. Soon he and eight other members of the Convention were writing a constitution for the new republic.

He did not foresee that the revolution was just beginning

and that soon much of what it had accomplished would be drowned in blood.

Nor did he realize that a radical group called the Jacobins was plotting to take over the government, led by such men of violence as Robespierre, Marat, and Danton. With his friend La Fayette and other liberals, he hoped that the overthrow of Louis XVI and the establishment of the Republic could be done peacefully. What happened instead was the Reign of Terror.

La Fayette then was commander of the National Guard, which had replaced the royal army. As such, he was responsible for keeping King Louis XVI and his queen, Marie Antoinette, under guard at the Tuileries, the palace in Paris to which they had been transferred from Versailles.

Early one morning, while Paine was still in bed, La Fayette rushed into his room with bad news.

The whitefaced young La Fayette announced, "The King is gone, the Queen and family with him, and no one knows where!"

"How did that happen?"

"All we know is that they slipped out of the Tuileries, the King disguised as a valet and the Queen as a governess. They fled in a royal coach and are believed to be heading for the German border. I have armed horsemen in pursuit on all the roads leading from Paris."

"It might be a good thing if they got away," Paine said. "Then the National Convention won't have to decide what to do with them. If they leave France of their own will, it will allow us to proceed with establishing a republic."

"But the Jacobins will blame me for letting them escape

when I had nothing to do with it," La Fayette said. "As a nobleman I am suspected of being secretly in sympathy with the royal family. The Jacobins are whispering, I am told, that I am in league with the King's sympathizers and plotting to keep the King on the throne."

La Fayette need not have worried, because the King and Queen were recaptured and brought back to Paris a few days later. A huge crowd gathered outside the Tuileries. It became an enraged mob, whipped to a fury by Jacobin orators, and began screaming for the King's and Queen's deaths. Paine himself was almost mobbed when someone in the crowd noticed that he wasn't wearing a tricolor cockade, the symbol of the Revolution.

It was obvious that the Jacobins were gaining power when the National Convention took up the matter of what to do with the King and Queen. The Jacobins said they should be sent to the guillotine and beheaded.

Paine, as one of the deputies, argued against the death penalty. "Kill the king but not the man," he pleaded before the National Convention. "Exile him to America where he can see how free men live. . . . The penalty of death should be abolished."

But the Convention ignored his plea. King and Queen were sent to the guillotine, and that was the beginning of the Reign of Terror. The Revolution all but destroyed itself. Of the nine men who drew up the first constitution, only Paine and one other man survived.

"At any hour," Paine told his French friends, "I expect my own neck to be placed under the knife. In England I am an outlaw. Only in America would I be safe."

On one October day alone, twelve deputies belonging to

the Girondin (the moderate) party, of which Paine was a member, were executed on the guillotine. Another day twenty-two other Girondists were hauled off the floor of the National Convention, taken to prison, and most of them put to death.

All, in fact, who had voted against death for Louis and Marie Antoinette, were marked for imprisonment or death by the Jacobins. Paine himself was being openly charged with being an English spy. That he had been sentenced to death in England, the Jacobins said, was only a pretense.

Paine wrote Thomas Jefferson that he once had hoped that through the French Revolution there had been "a good prospect of extending liberty throughout the greatest part of Europe," but "I now relinquish that hope."

Even as he walked in danger day and night, he was working on another book, to be called *The Age of Reason,* which his enemies were to call "The Devil's Prayer Book." In it he expressed the hope for a triumph of reason and intelligence over ignorance and superstition. He wrote the book, as he explained in a letter to Samuel Adams, because the French people were "running headlong into atheism" and he wanted to "fix them to the first article of every man's creed who has any creed at all. . . . *I believe in God."* Creation, he emphasized in the book, was the "ever-existing word of God. . . . It proclaims His power, it demonstrates His wisdom, it manifests His goodness and beneficence."

As he worked on that manuscript in his rooms in the Faubourg St. Denis he expected at any moment that a squad of police would break in and take him to prison. Yet his main concern wasn't for his own safety but for his manuscript of *The Age of Reason.*

"If you hear of my being arrested," he told Joel Barlow, a young American friend living in Paris, "come quickly. I want you to take my manuscript and see to its being published."

"Surely," Barlow said, "the American representatives in Paris will see to it that you are released if that happens."

Paine gave him a twisted smile. "You think so?" he asked. "And who is now the American minister to France? Gouverneur Morris. He has never really forgiven me for my part in the Silas Deane Affair, though he has been my guest and I have been his. Morris would do nothing to help me."

At four o'clock on the morning of December 28, 1793, a squad of police came to Paine's quarters, got him out of bed, and placed him under arrest. He had been charged with being an enemy of the Revolution. The police granted his request that they wait for Barlow to take charge of the manuscript of *The Age of Reason* before imprisoning Paine.

Paine was taken to Luxembourg Prison, and there he stayed month after month. It was a place of horror, filled with the cries of those who had the "cross of death" marked on their cell doors and were then removed to the guillotine. Paine's cell was damp and the food was rotten. His body was covered with sores which would not heal. Then he came down with a fever which caused spells of delirium and unconsciousness.

Gouverneur Morris meanwhile was making little effort to obtain his freedom, though Paine was legally a citizen of the United States. He simply refused to apply pressure on the French for Paine's release.

The excuse that Morris used in a letter to Jefferson, apparently in reply to the latter's query about what was being done for Paine, was that the prisoner's life might be endangered if the matter was brought to the attention of the French government. "If he is quiet in prison," Morris wrote Jefferson, "he may have the good luck to be forgotten, whereas should he be brought much into notice, the long suspended axe might fall on him. I believe he thinks that I ought to claim him as an American citizen, but considering his birth, his naturalization in this country, and the place he filled, I doubt much the right. . . ."

Nothing Morris could say, however, made Paine any less an American citizen. He had never given up his United States citizenship. The French citizenship conferred on him was also given, as an honor, to Washington, Madison, Hamilton, and other heroes of the American Revolution. But the title "Citizen Tom Paine" was one Paine valued highly.

Americans then living in Paris, disgusted at Morris' refusal to help Paine, drew up an appeal to the government then headed by the bloody fanatic Robespierre. Thousands were being killed on suspicion of opposing his Reign of Terror.

Any night might be Paine's last on earth. One evening orders were issued for 182 inmates of Luxembourg Prison to be executed on the guillotine the following morning. Paine was among those condemned. Somehow the wardens overlooked the "cross of death" chalked on his cell door, and by sheer luck Paine escaped the guillotine.

The summer of 1794, when Paine had been in prison for more than six months, Morris was suddenly recalled to America and James Monroe was sent to replace him as Minister to France. Monroe had known Paine ever since the early days of the American Revolution, when Monroe was a young officer on Washington's staff.

By the time Monroe had arrived, Paine's hair had turned white and he was a ghostly figure, thin, pale, and sick. He barely had strength enough to write Monroe a letter appealing for his help and pointing out that he had twice taken the oath of allegiance to America.

With all the vigor and force at his command, Monroe set about trying to secure Paine's release. That was not easy, since the French government was in a state of confusion following the execution of Robespierre. Monroe wrote a series of letters to the Committee of General Safety, which was more or less in charge of the political prisoners, declaring that Paine was an American citizen and the French had no right to keep him in prison. Almost three months passed before Monroe's constant pressure was successful.

On November 4, 1794—exactly ten months and nine days after he was arrested—Monroe learned that Paine would be released and went to Luxembourg Prison in his carriage.

The door of the prison courtyard swung open, and Paine tottered out, barely able to walk, looking like a man of ninety rather than his real age of fifty-seven.. Monroe hurried over to help Paine into his carriage, which took them to the Monroe residence.

Monroe, who was to be the fourth President of the United States, and his wife nursed Paine and obtained the best available doctors to treat him. Food and rest improved his condition within a few weeks, but then he had a relapse and it looked as though he might die. Monroe wrote to a friend at home that "the prospect now is that he will not be able to hold out more than a month or two. . . ." Under the Monroes' care, however, he slowly got better and recovered his strength. But from then on his health would be poor.

While still confined to bed, he worked on the final chapters of *The Age of Reason,* on his autobiography, and on a history of the American Revolution which Benjamin Franklin had urged him to undertake.

The publication of *The Age of Reason* caused an uproar in England and America and brought charges that he was an atheist, even though he plainly stated his belief in "one God and no more." It was the churches and clergy who were chiefly offended, because he was outspoken against organized religion. They also believed there was more to pleasing God than Paine's definition of that duty as "doing justice, loving mercy, and endeavoring to make our fellow creatures happy."

When he regained his strength, he moved from the Monroes' home to the home of a young French couple, Nicolas and Marguerite Bonneville, and their three small children. The Bonnevilles had been his friends ever since he came to Paris, Nicolas being a writer and editor himself. In their home Paine continued writing and campaigning for the release of the Marquis de La Fayette and his wife, who were in prison as accused enemies of the Revolution. He also continued his career as a deputy to the National Convention, to which he was restored in 1795.

He spent much time brooding over the fact that George Washington, now President, had made no apparent attempt to obtain his release from the Luxembourg Prison. Paine puzzled over that for months. In the past Washington had always befriended and defended him. Yet the President had not lifted a finger to get Paine out of the French prison.

Was it, he wondered, because Washington was then trying to negotiate a treaty with England by which the British would withdraw their forces from a number of military posts they still occupied south of the Great Lakes? England was pleased that Paine was in prison and might have been annoyed if Washington tried to get him out.

Or had Washington grown so self-important in the Presidency that he couldn't be bothered with helping an old friend?

Or now that he was in power, had Washington acquired a distaste for all revolutionaries? Washington had taken up with the Federalists, who in Paine's opinion believed property was more important than people.

The more he thought about Washington's neglect— which has never been explained, only guessed at—the angrier Paine became. He wrote a letter to the President, in which he charged that "you folded your arms, forgot your friend, and became silent." But James Monroe persuaded him not to send it.

Months later Paine wrote another letter, and this was

sent. "I shall continue to think of you as treacherous," he wrote Washington, "until you give me cause to think otherwise." It was not answered.

Paine then published an angrily worded pamphlet titled *Letter to George Washington,* which harmed him more than its target. By now Washington was secure forever in the hearts of his countrymen. He all but accused Washington of having betrayed the American Revolution, and that was something very few Americans were prepared to believe. It would have been wiser to swallow his sense of betrayal, in the realization that men are shaped by power and that Washington might have considered an agreement with England more important than one ex-comrade's life, but Paine could never ignore an injustice.

For the next five years he lived, fairly comfortably, with Marguerite and Nicolas Bonneville and their children at 4, Rue du Théâtre Français. Often, however, he was assailed by yearnings to return to America, where he still owned the farm at New Rochelle and the house at Bordentown. Both properties were rented and brought him a small income. France and England were at war, however, and he could not risk being captured by a British ship which would have taken him in chains to be hanged on an English gallows.

During the several years following his release from prison, Paine became one of Paris' most famous citizens. His writings, rather than his political activities, made him known to almost everyone capable of reading a book.

One of those attracted by that fame was the young General Napoleon Bonaparte, who came to the Bonneville house one day to meet and discuss *Rights of Man* with its author. The Corsican, who had recently returned from victories with the French army in Italy, claimed to be interested in Paine's ideas on human rights. They had a number of meetings, but eventually Paine saw that the ambitious young general was trying to use him.

"A statue of gold should be erected to you in every city of the universe," Napoleon told Paine.

Soon, however, he was suggesting that when France invaded England, as Napoleon was urging, Paine should come along to help persuade the English people they were being liberated. And Paine could see that Napoleon was hoping to use him to further his military ambitions. He decided that Napoleon was a trickster who "wants only power, conquest, and bloodshed."

The friendship soon withered.

"*My Heart Grows Cold . . .*"

I I

HOMESICK and still ailing from his months in prison, Paine wrote Thomas Jefferson, now President of the United States, that he wanted to return to America. On March 18, 1801, President Jefferson replied that he hoped Paine would come home soon. "I am in hopes," Jefferson added, "you will find us returned generally to sentiments worthy of former times. In these it will be your glory to have steadily labored, and with as much effect as any man living. That you may long live to continue your useful labors . . . is my sincere prayer."

It would be another year before Paine managed to leave. He wanted the Bonnevilles to come with him. They had become "his" family. Nicolas and Marguerite were like a son and daughter to him, their three children like grandchildren.

Nicolas Bonneville had published a newspaper, *Bien Informé,* in which he called General Napoleon Bonaparte "another Cromwell" because of his military and political ambitions. The paper was closed down, and Bonneville was imprisoned. After he was released, he was considered a suspicious person and was watched by the secret police and barely made a living out of translating foreign articles into French.

One day he returned to the house in the Rue du Théâtre Français with bad news for Paine and his family.

"I have been told by the authorities that I will not be permitted to leave the country," he told them. "Besides we do not have the money to pay for our passage. It is best that you leave without us, Tom, and we will join you when we can."

"I have money for your passage," Paine said.

"But what would I do, how could I make a living in a strange country?" Bonneville asked.

"I have enough money to provide for everything," Paine answered. "You are a bright young man and will find your footing soon enough."

"It's no use to talk about it," Bonneville said, "as long as the authorities won't let me leave France."

"They'll change their mind," Paine declared. "Send Marguerite and the children on ahead, and join us when you can."

So it was decided. Paine himself landed in America late in October, 1802. It was almost a year later when Marguerite Bonneville and her children arrived. Her husband was not permitted to leave France, but the family, with Paine's help, settled themselves in America.

Jefferson and other friends were glad to see Paine back in the country he helped to liberate. On landing in Baltimore, Paine had journeyed directly to Washington, D.C., now the capital of the United States. Even before he arrived in Washington, however, the anti-Jefferson newspapers were showering Paine with abuse, and along with him the President himself. One called him a "lying, drunken, brutal infidel." Another boldly declared that "Jefferson and his blasphemous crony should dangle from the same gallows."

During the fifteen years of his absence, Paine found, America had changed. The power of money was greater than before. Revolutionary ideals of liberty and equality had been forgotten. And there was a bitter fight going on between the Federalists, the party of Washington and Adams, which wanted the wealthy to control the government, and the republicans, like Jefferson and Monroe, who believed in personal liberty and human rights. The "sentiments worthy of former times" which Jefferson had mentioned in his letter to Paine a year earlier, were slow in developing.

Paine and the President spent many hours together in Washington, and Paine was offered a post in the government. Paine turned down the offer because he was sixty-five years old and wanted to devote his remaining years to his writing.

A little more than two weeks after he returned to this country, Paine was writing in a Washington paper, the *National Intelligencer,* of his disappointment in what the United States was becoming. In Europe the "dawn of liberty was rising" but its "lustre was fading in America,"

[*115*]

and he believed that the "principles of the Revolution were expiring on the soil that produced them."

This was the first of a series of what he called *Letters to Citizens of the United States*. In the second he attacked ex-President John Adams for having royalist inclinations. In the third he charged that his enemies in America, "these Terrorists of the New World," were "waiting in the devotion of their hearts for the joyful news of my destruction" when Robespierre had him thrown into the French prison.

Much as he had yearned to return to America, Paine was restless and dissatisfied with what he saw. On leaving the nation's new capital, he stopped at Bordentown to visit his old friend, Colonel Kirkbride, and then looked over his farm at New Rochelle.

He was living in New York City when Marguerite Bonneville and her children arrived in America. At first he arranged for them to live in his cottage at Bordentown, then they moved to lodgings near his own in New York while Mrs. Bonneville taught French to private pupils.

In 1804, Paine and the Bonneville family moved to the New Rochelle farm when his tenant's lease expired. They stayed there less than a year, however, because the house was extremely cold in the winter.

The rest of his life, becoming more obscure with each passing year, Paine spent in various boarding houses in Greenwich Village. Mrs. Bonneville and her children lived nearby. She taught French and in her spare time looked after Paine as best she could. Her husband, for some reason which historians have never been able to unearth, stayed in France even after a change of government would have permitted him to rejoin his family.

In his late sixties, living mostly on bread and rum, Paine was a lonely and embittered man whose health would never recover from his months of imprisonment in France. From time to time he wrote articles or letters expressing his hatred of what was happening to the American Republic.

The continuation of slavery—its increase, in fact, as the Louisiana Purchase opened up millions of acres for cotton plantations—was particularly hard for Paine to bear in silence. He had spoken out against slavery long before America won her independence, and believed it would be the nation's ruin if it was not soon abolished. "Had I the command of the elements I would blast Liverpool with fire and brimstone," he wrote, because that English port was the center of the slave trade.

He was also disappointed when Congress refused to pass his claim for money he spent in going to France as Colonel Laurens' advisor.

"After so many years of service," he said, "my heart grows cold towards America."

One of his few friends aside from the Bonneville family was a Quaker watchmaker named Willett Hicks, who often visited him in the boarding house at 59 Grove Street. Through Hicks, he asked that he be buried in the Quaker burial ground, but the Quakers refused because they didn't like what he wrote about religion in *The Age of Reason*.

Early in 1809, when he was close to his seventy-second birthday, he became seriously ill. He was gaunt and shrunken and feverish, but his wit still had a cutting edge.

"Your belly diminishes," his doctor observed one day while visiting the old man. Dr. Romayne had a large stomach.

"And yours," Paine snapped back, "augments."

One day close to the end, he called Mrs. Bonneville to his room and announced that he had made out his will. He read the document, which directed that the farm at New Rochelle be sold and half the proceeds go to his English friend, Thomas Clio Rickman, and the other half to the Bonnevilles.

"I want your children to be properly educated," Paine explained. "Perhaps, if I'd had more schooling, I would have done better in life, been wiser and more discreet."

"Nonsense," Mrs. Bonneville commented. "You are a great man, even if the world has mostly forgotten."

"Ah, yes," Paine replied, "look how I am surrounded by friends, admirers, and well-wishers on my death-bed."

"You will be remembered," she said firmly.

"Yes, as a common scold to humanity. But never mind. Listen to the rest of my will. . . . 'I desire to be buried in a square of twelve feet, to be enclosed with rows of trees, and a stone or post or rail fence, with a headstone with my name and age engraved upon it, author of *Common Sense.*' There, my dear, at least I will have some privacy when I am dead."

In his last days, Mrs. Bonneville and his Quaker friend, Willett Hicks, were at his bedside constantly. No one else paid much attention to the old man dying in a Greenwich Village boarding house. The new generation, born long after the Revolution ended, knew of him as a pamphleteer and associate of Washington, but had little idea of his true importance. "A mere scribbler," his surviving political enemies called him.

On the morning of June 8, 1809, he died peacefully in his sleep at the age of seventy-two.

The death was noted by only one of the dozen New York newspapers. "Died on Thursday, the 8th instant, Thomas Paine, author of *Crisis, Rights of Man,* etc.," the *Evening Post* briefly reported. "Mr. Paine had a desire to be interred in the Quaker burying ground and some days previous to his demise had an interview with some Quaker gentlemen on the subject, but . . . his anxious wishes were not complied with. . . . He had lived long, done some good, and much harm."

His funeral was no occasion for public mourning. It was, in fact, little noticed. Only half a dozen persons accompanied the body to New Rochelle for the burial on his farm—Mrs. Bonneville and her three children (one of whom, Major General Benjamin Bonneville, later fought in the Mexican and Civil Wars), two Negroes (Currier and Johnstone), and the faithful Quaker Willett Hicks.

On the way to New Rochelle, an Englishman asked the mourners whose funeral it was. Tom Paine's, replied Hicks.

"Paine did a lot of mischief in the world," the Englishman remarked, "and if there is a purgatory he will certainly have a good share of it before the devil lets him go."

"On that score," Hicks replied, "I would sooner take my chance with Paine than any man in New York."

With those half dozen of the faithful gathered around, Paine was buried on his farm at New Rochelle. There was

[*119*]

no religious service.   The only words spoken were Mrs. Bonneville's:

"Oh, Mr. Paine," she said in a trembling voice, "my sons stand here as testimony of the gratitude of America, and I for France."

Even in death Tom Paine was not safe from his public. Ten years after his death an English admirer named William Cobbett secretly went to the Paine farm, dug up Paine's remains, and took them to England for burial. Cobbett intended to raise a large fund by subscription and create a shrine for Paine, whom he considered a martyr. His project was greeted with laughter and sneers, was joked about in the comic papers.   Paine had been dead long enough to be forgotten by America, for which he fought, but not by England, which he fought against. Cobbett kept Paine's bones until his death, then they passed into other hands, and simply disappeared.   Where they finally came to rest, no one knows.

Equally grim was the fate of his unpublished works, principally his autobiography—which should have been fascinating, one of the great documents of his time—and his history of the American Revolution, which probably would have destroyed more than one stately reputation. They were left in the care of Mrs. Bonneville, but were destroyed when a fire swept the attic in which she kept them.

His published work, and the story of his life, survive as the testament of a great and selfless American.   No man of his time, except Washington, Jefferson, and Franklin, is more honored today. His books are still read by millions all over the world. He was the father of the idea that every man is entitled to liberty, that protecting his freedom is the state's first duty. Wherever that idea is in danger, Tom Paine still stands guard.

Index

About the Author and Artist

Richard O'Connor is a former newspaperman with a host of writing credits. He is well-known as a biographer and has won much praise from reviewers. The *Library Journal* said of his biography SITTING BULL, "A thought-provoking account of the white man's treatment of the Indians and of a great Sioux Chief. . . ." His juveniles—YOUNG BAT MASTERSON, SITTING BULL, and JOHN LLOYD STEPHENS—have been published by McGraw-Hill. Mr. O'Connor lives in Ellsworth, Maine.

Richard Cuffari is a graduate of Pratt Institute and for a number of years has been an illustrator of children's books. The Society of Illustrators has awarded him Certificates of Merit in their annual shows. He and his family live in Brooklyn, New York.